The Tao of Right and Wrong

The Tao of Right and Wrong

Rediscovering Humanity's Moral Foundations

Dennis Danielson

REGENT COLLEGE PUBLISHING
Vancouver, British Columbia

Regent College Publishing
5800 University Boulevard
Vancouver, BC V6T 2E4 Canada
www.regentpublishing.com

Regent College Publishing is an imprint of the Regent Bookstore (www.regentbookstore.com). Views expressed in works published by Regent College Publishing are those of the author and do not necessarily represent the official position of Regent College (www.regent-college.edu).

ISBN 978-1-57383-540-4

Cataloguing in Publication information is available from Library and Archives Canada.

Cover image art by Xiaofeng Wu
Jacket design by Daniela Amestegui

For Ebba

Contents

Preface

Have you ever heard yourself saying things like "Mary is *such* a good person"? Or have you ever thought, after hearing about "collateral damage" when an army mounted an attack that in the process killed children and other civilians, "That's just *so* wrong"? Or have you ever, as a child or an adult, been cheated out of something rightfully yours—a favor, a possession, a promotion—and responded with "That's just *so* unfair"?

If you have, then whether you've called them this in so many words, you've uttered *moral judgments*: calling things or people or actions good or bad, right or wrong. We all do it all the time. And we do it not because we're "judgmental" or mora*listic* or self-righteous people, but because to *exercise* moral judgment is part of how we think about and respond to the world—part of how we function as human beings. Yes, we can sometimes be mistaken in those judgments. Something can happen to make you change your mind about Mary. Or you might discover evidence that reveals you weren't cheated after all. To make a moral judgment isn't the same as being dogmatic, or closing your eyes or your mind to evidence that might cause you to revise that judgment. But when you do make it, when you say "Mary is a good person," you are describing something other than just warm fuzzy feelings you happen to have about Mary. You are describing Mary, a real person; you are saying something significant about her. And if somebody comes along and tells you "That's just your opinion," you might well reply, politely, "It *is* my opinion, but it's not *just* my opinion. Here are my reasons for thinking that Mary *is* a good person." You might carry on to defend your judgment as accurate, reasonable, and true. I certainly hope you would.

That's what this little book is about. It sketches a case for the cogency and rightness of a *realistic* understanding of morality, a case today often ignored, neglected, even undermined in Western society generally, but particularly in our schools. It is a compact introduction—an essay or "primer"—that I hope renders moral realism clearer to you whether you're a student, a teacher, a parent, or perhaps none of these things. My topic is the foundation, nature, and practical exercise of morality in relation to education and human knowledge, with a focus on central questions that concern everyone: What makes a person a good person? What is just? What is right? What is wrong? What purposes, and what virtues, are worth pursuing? How can we meaningfully weigh responses to such questions—honest responses that you yourself make—without these being dismissed as "just your opinion"? At stake in such great issues is the very meaning of our language and our lives, the shaping of our characters, and the future of our families and our culture.

So my aim is to put the argument for moral realism as a challenge for twenty-first-century thought and life. Particularly in educational and political systems in which ethical claims—statements about right and wrong, "shoulds" and "oughts"—are so often assumed to be fundamentally either socially or culturally "constructed" or else purely individual and subjective matters, we need a surer footing than the shifting sands of moral relativism. To put it even more starkly, we require an escape from moral nihilism. If, in our schools and culture, we still hope somehow to cultivate virtuous human beings, citizens of character, men and women of high purpose, then we need a trenchant critique of subjectivism and the "that's-just-your-opinion" school of thought, a critique that can serve as an antidote to a virus threatening to paralyze us both individually and collectively.

In reframing the case for moral realism, as well as in my title, I employ a useful piece of vocabulary borrowed from C. S. Lewis's *The Abolition of Man*: the *Tao*, which serves as shorthand for the trans-cultural fund or "reservoir" of teachings that is the source of moral judgment, of codes of ethics, and of standards of right and wrong. The word bespeaks something universal. And while it obviously derives its form and part of its meaning from Chinese philosophy, it is not intended to evoke Taoism as such. Its role will become clearer over the course of the book's three chapters, and I hope it helps us rediscover an essential component of our humanity. I aim, in addition, to offer fresh insights and examples that speak to the thought-world in which we find ourselves. Over the past half century, broad moral realism has been enriched by what's known as "virtue ethics," and I hope to fortify my argument with some of the wisdom that this approach offers.

My goal, however, is directly to *illustrate and support* moral realism rather than to pursue an academic discussion *about* morality or moral philosophy. If you are interested in exploring the much wider philosophical discussion, you might carry on by tracing threads left loose in my endnotes, or by sampling items listed in the short "Further Reading" section at the end of the book. Or you can simply dip into works cited in the Appendix, "Illustrations of the *Tao*"—intended to extend and deepen our acquaintance with moral realism by excerpting specific ethical teachings embodied in a broad range of traditions: Greek, Egyptian, Roman, Hindu, Hebrew, Christian, Buddhist, Confucian, Islamic, Old Norse, Old English, North American Indigenous, and Sikh.

So may *The Tao of Right and Wrong* help reawaken the present generation to the riches and the reality of humanity's moral foundations.

1

Humans Without Hearts

Almost anyone who has gone through elementary and secondary school treasures memories of at least one teacher who has shaped and influenced them in positive ways that go beyond imparting bare knowledge of a certain subject. I am no exception, and nothing I say here is intended to disrespect the efforts and genuine accomplishments of teachers devoted to educating young people.

Instead, the target of my critique in this chapter is what often underlies the curriculum that teachers are required to teach. For it is an urgent matter for our communities and our democracy that we understand, and that we demand to know, what kinds of morals—what notions about right and wrong—our schools instill in our children, often at a very early age, and what kinds of reasons the young are given for being virtuous people and good citizens. If we examine standard curricula mandated by governments and school boards around the English-

1

speaking world, the picture that emerges is a discouraging one.

Today, the dominant assumptions and de facto orthodoxies about morality are thoroughly relativistic: Judgments about right and wrong are, standard curricula suggest, determined merely by our biology, or by our cultures (and of course there are many), or by our individual or collective emotions or subjectivities—or by some combination of these factors. The key phrase here is "determined merely by . . . " Nobody would be so foolhardy as to argue that biology or culture or emotions are irrelevant to our moral judgments. The problem arises, however, when we treat these things, either one-by-one or in combination, as exclusive determinants of right and wrong. In this regard, a common fallacy is to recognize that we humans are powerfully shaped by nature and nurture, but then to slip into the presumption that morality—judgments or claims concerning right and wrong—can't be connected with, or rooted in, anything transcending nature and nurture.[1]

In Chapter 2 we'll consider some of the ways that biological and cultural relativisms fail to offer a satisfactory basis for morality. But here, let's cut straight to some of the things students are actually taught in school that impede our capacity to think realistically about moral issues, things that subjectivize and trivialize ethical statements and undermine the very virtues we might properly consider part of any education worthy of the name. Although I doubt most educators deliberately aim to teach their students that statements expressing moral judgments are unimportant, many standard materials currently required promote that conclusion. A crucial item among such materials sounds at first innocent enough. For example, the official curriculum of my home province of British Columbia—titled "Building Student Success"—has a section on "competencies" to be acquired in English Language Arts (in this case as taught to eleven- and twelve-year-olds). This document mandates that "students should be prompted to distinguish fact from opinion." Similar language appears in the Common Core Curriculum currently adopted for use in schools in over forty states in the U.S. In History/Social Studies 6–12, the "Reading Standards for Literacy" state that students must acquire an ability to "distinguish among fact, opinion, and reasoned judgment in a text."

How could anyone object to something that sounds so reasonable? The problem arises when we examine teaching materials—definitions, worksheets with separate columns for facts and opinions, instructional videos, and the like—that actually accompany the Common Core and other curricula like it. Some examples are more egregious than others. A standard definition of "fact," according to such curricula, declares that it is a statement that can be proven. Some materials go so far as to assert that facts may be true or false,[2] which makes a nonsense of what most

English-speakers mean by "fact." (Imagine having an argument in which you claim something is a fact, and your opponent says "Yes, I agree it's a fact, but it's a false fact.") Not all teaching materials make this blunder, although another claim in some instructional videos is that a fact "is always true." We needn't waste time here over such incoherent claims, despite how confusing they must be for students wishing to understand the concept of "fact." Among obvious counterexamples is the factual claim "I am twelve years old"—which may be provable now but wasn't true last year and won't be true next year.

A further problem with the definition of fact as something that's provable is that it can convey a false sense of how easy it is to establish what *is* factual. Whether in history, or law, or science, some of human beings' greatest intellectual challenges—some extending over years, even centuries—have involved attempts to discern and to prove what is truly the case. To mention only one famous example from the history of science, Copernicus's claim that the earth revolves about the sun rather than the other way around took roughly a hundred and fifty years to establish demonstratively. It was no straightforward matter of marshalling scientific fact against mere opinion.[3] To suggest that things we call "facts" don't entail controversy or require interpretation is seriously misleading. Current lessons about facts as taught by the Common Core (and elsewhere) appear even more uninformed and incoherent when we consider that our everyday usage emerged bare-ly three hundred years ago. We "take facts so much for granted," writes one prominent historian, that we may be surprised to learn they are indeed "a modern invention."[4]

And what about the definition of opinion? Disting-uished from facts, opinions (in the language of the Common Core) are most obviously statements that *can't* be proven. Students are taught to watch out for certain vocabulary that characterizes such statements: words like "good," "bad," and "should." Most "opinions" cited in mate-rials linked with the Common Core appear uncontrover-sial if stunningly banal, indeed trivial. Repeated examples include "Dogs make better pets than cats" and "Chocolate ice cream tastes better than vanilla." Much more disturb-ing, however, is the way that judgments about value or morals are also mixed in with preferences of ice-cream fla-vors and defined as opinions (and by suggestion *merely as* opinions). One set of exercises offering a paragraph about the ancient construction of the pyramids at Giza in Egypt asks students to classify statements as fact, opinion, or fact and opinion. One sentence reads "To build the pyramids, thousands of laborers worked under unfair, brutal condi-tions." The indicated correct response is that the statement is a combination of fact and opinion—with presumably the large number of laborers being factual, and their un-fair, brutal conditions being merely a matter of opinion. I suspect that among those laborers it might have been a unanimous opinion! But today's students are taught, when they're studying history, that the really important thing to look for is the facts.

As already illustrated by a few examples, teaching materials such as those related to the Common Core frequently offer students little guidance in distinguishing between facts and factual *statements*. This failure might help explain the muddles mentioned earlier about "true and false facts," since factual *claims* can be true or false, whereas "fact" implies truth. There's also confusion between *provable* and true. A factual claim may be true even if we can't (or can't yet) prove it—and after all, what human beings really want to know is the truth, not just "the facts," even if there's a big overlap between these categories.

Most corrosive, however, is the confusion that the simplistic and philosophically shallow binary classification of fact and opinion entails for moral judgment—not for "moralistic judgmentalism" but for the kind of judgment you express when you declare that Mary is a good person or that it's wrong to injure an opposing player so that your team can win a game. In the teaching materials of the Common Core, statements such as "copying homework assignments is wrong" and "All men are created equal" are relegated to the domain of mere opinion, and claims of right and wrong are placed at the level of subjective preferences for one flavor of ice cream over another. Students may accordingly think they're studying

English or history, but the lesson they absorb is that right and wrong are subjective, and that statements about such matters are "personal," just like assertions that dogs make better pets than cats.[5]

Of course I do not say "consciously absorb." Perhaps the greatest danger of the kinds of teaching illustrated here is that its recipients are (many of them) eleven- or twelve-year-olds, not young adults—children supposedly being taught English Language Arts, or History and Social Studies, without any awareness "that ethics, theology, and politics are all at stake." What's being put into students' minds is "not a theory ... but an assumption" that in ten years will condition them "to take one side in a contro-versy [they have] never recognized as a controversy at all."[6] Alasdair MacIntyre sums up this assumption under what he calls "emotivism": "the doctrine that all evaluative judgments and more specifically all moral judgments are nothing but expressions of preference, expressions of atti-tude or feeling. ... [Furthermore,] moral judgments, being expressions of attitude or feeling, are neither true nor false; and agreement in moral judgment is not to be secured by any rational method." As MacIntyre puts it, this view "has become embodied in our culture," a process that "marks a degeneration, a grave cultural loss."[7]

If educators themselves truly accepted the relegation of "shoulds" and "oughts"—and judgments about what is important—to the status of uncertain and unprovable opinion or statements of attitude, then there would be no point in our trying to convince them of the "bad" effects of the kind of teaching materials sketched so far, for that conclusion would itself be a value judgment (words like "good," "bad," and "important," of course, marking any such claim as mere opinion). The glaring contradictions, however, between our schools' curricula and their own statements of purpose, learning principles, and codes of conduct might raise the suspicion that today's educators don't actually believe—and at least some of them don't put into practice—the fact-vs.-opinion materials they're required to teach.

For example, as mentioned earlier, the official curriculum of British Columbia, which asserts that "students should be prompted to distinguish fact from opinion," bears the title "Building Student Success." Even passing over the fact that the document employs a "should" statement, we might have difficulty imagining a thoroughgoing definition of student success that avoids still further value judgments—markers of good success or poor success. The Ministry of Education in another Canadian province, Ontario, states explicitly in its Code of Conduct that "A school should be a place that promotes responsibility, respect, civility, and academic excellence."[8] Who could disagree with such a claim? Yet it's almost impossible—given prevalent distinctions between fact and opinion—not to worry that mandated qualities such as respect and excellence themselves fall into the inferior category of mere opinion.

Schools' and education ministries' statements of purpose and codes of conduct often betray embarrassment, however, at their own implicit use of value judgments. Such embarrassment at openly ethical language results in contorted attempts to find other vocabulary that obscures what in truth is an appeal to moral standards. Anybody who has spent time in the educational system in the past twenty years or so might have noticed the prevalence of word pairs such as positive-and-negative, appropriate-and-inappropriate, to describe students' behaviors, attitudes, and educational results.

Some efforts to endorse morality without using moral language verge on self-parody. According to an official document on student conduct in the Australian state of Victoria, "Positive student behaviours are most effectively developed and supported through relationship-based whole-school and classroom practices, and clearly communicated behavioural expectations." Seeking clarification of such bureaucratese, we read down the page and find an account of certain "challenging" (and evidently less-than-positive) behaviors that students are discouraged from exhibiting. These include "**Disruptive behaviours** such as ... tantrums, swearing, screaming or refusing to follow instructions"; "**Violent and/or unsafe behaviours** such as head banging, kicking, biting, punching, fighting, running away, smashing equipment or furniture"; and "**Inappropriate social behaviours** such as ... stealing, being over-affectionate, inappropriate touching or masturbation." None of these behaviors is actually said to be wrong; certainly no reasons are given for calling them wrong. They're simply "challenging," "inappropriate," and by implication "negative," placing school authorities and particularly teachers in a position of having to communicate clearly that such things are contrary to "expectations." Of course we're left to ask "Whose expectations?" At one level, given how detailed their lists of transgressions are, it sounds as if the documents' authors *do* expect the challenging behaviors! Moreover, the same document places enormous pressure on teachers to avoid "triggering" challenging behaviors on the part of students, and also of course to avoid any "boring or disorganised lessons, [or] over-reaction to misbehaviour."[9]

Such examples illustrate how educational experts and authorities have apparently become entangled in their own fact-opinion ideology, the one taught to students throughout our school systems—and also how truly inept and muddled are their applications of it. For *of course* educators must base their practices and "expectations" on convictions about what is right and wrong. Moral principles are foundational for what we aim to do when we educate children and cultivate good citizens and mature human beings. But our embarrassment about frank expressions of morality serves to cut off the branch we're sitting on.

Imagine some smart student bent on exhibiting "challenging" behaviors—head banging, smashing school equipment, stealing, and so on—who demands *why* such behaviors are not permitted, *why* they are deemed "inappropriate." The honest, truthful answer surely will be some form of "They're basically wrong." According to the fact-opinion dichotomy, however, that answer is not itself factual; it's just somebody's opinion. In the words of the APEL Education Consultancy firm, "it is important to recognize whether [conclusions] are based on solid evidence. ... What is the difference between a fact and an opinion? A fact is a piece of information that can be strictly defined and proved true. An opinion is a statement that expresses a belief, value, or feeling. An opinion cannot be proved true or false."[10] Such statements are self-defeating. They tell us what's important (itself a value judgment!) and then declare that value-statements fall into the inferior category of mere opinion. And unless school authorities refuse that premise, they (knowingly or not) eviscerate their own codes of conduct.

Even if we can't decisively answer the question, it's worth pausing to ask why educators, and to a large extent the rest of us, have grown so squeamish in the presence of words like "right" and "wrong." Why do we resort to euphemisms like "positive," "negative," "appropriate," "inappropriate," "challenging," and the like? Why does openly moral language make us as uneasy as a Victorian asked to discuss the details of human reproduction?

No doubt many of us shy away from expressing moral judgments simply for fear of appearing "judgmental." Apart from the irony of claiming that a judgmental posture is *wrong*, the pendulum may simply have swung away from hurtful, dogmatic, or culturally myopic forms of judgment. Well and good. Others have perhaps felt that the best way of avoiding dogmatism, moralism, judgmentalism, and authoritarianism is to adopt a thoroughgoing uncertainty about moral principles. We might charitably even think of this as a kind of humility. In any case, I suspect, such are among the nobler motives behind our reticence to use moral language.

Another, less noble, but still understandable explanation may have to do with the "myth of progress," as it's sometimes called. In the West and many other places in the world (although certainly not everywhere) human beings today enjoy on average better health, longer lives, more comfortable circumstances, and so on than they did in the past. Such improvements seem to support the easy blanket assumption that "now" is better than "back then." Sometimes it no doubt is, but that doesn't justify any wholesale affirmation of the superiority of the present state of things. Yet those of us who are no longer young know that one of the most devastating and unanswerable criticisms we can receive is that we're "old-fashioned" or "backward-looking." The very idea of a moral code can appear antiquated or parochial. And so perhaps we're afraid that, if we used openly moral language, we'd appear regressive and, again, intolerant. Nobody wants to appear a throwback.

As already argued, however, there's no avoiding certain kinds of moral intolerance. Innumerable institutions and firms today have found it necessary to state explicitly, for example, that bullying or workplace harassment won't be tolerated. My critique is not of such codes but of educational curricula that undermine—in both educators and their students—our very capacity to make such assertions about right and wrong with conviction and without embarrassment.

Another likely motivation for valorizing "fact" over "opinion" (as defined in the curricular material cited so far) is the perfectly legitimate desire of educators to strengthen young people against the undoubted allure of biased claims made on websites, in commercial advertising, in political or religious propaganda, and the like. Skills of "critical thinking" or "skeptical inquiry" unquestionably have important applications in this regard. We do not want to raise a generation of children who are easy prey to emotionalism or who lack the capacity to discern when politicians, advertisers, or charlatans are manipulating them for their own ends. To be useful, however, any solvent requires a container that is itself not dissolved by the solvent. And as we have seen, prevalent definitions of fact and opinion have the effect of burning a hole in educators' own capacity to affirm and uphold moral principles, principles whose denial is corrosive to proper and healthy human relations.

Any list of reasons for reticence concerning moral assertions would be incomplete without brief, if inadequate, mention of so-called postmodern philosophy. This relatively recent trend of thought places under suspicion any definite assertion, be it of fact or opinion. For in this view *all* claims to knowledge are contingent, relative, "constructed." So according to postmodern theory, even the notion of proof so beloved of fact-vs.-opinion proponents leaves us with the question "proven to whom?" And if proof is contingent upon its reception or affirmation by a particular public or audience, then supposed facts end up being just as radically subjective as opinions are. All knowledge is thus "situated" socially, culturally, linguistically, and so on. These are weighty claims—but also carry with them the risk of radical skepticism, even cynicism. Such skepticism threatens, again, the core of what makes us human, wielding a critique that undermines all moral judgments, reading them as "interested," so that all expressions of right can be translated into expressions of might, and all human relations are fundamentally power relations.[11]

~

As already suggested, however, to debunk or deconstruct a statement of value, belief, or conviction is quite easy even if you lack fluency in postmodern philosophy. All you need is our standard curricula with their simple division between facts and opinions. You tell me what you consider right, or good, or "positive," and I reply, "That's just your opinion"—and carry on smashing school furniture. No doubt somebody will intervene to stop me, but wouldn't it be better, more truly constructive, for educators to offer me—in place of a list of "challenging" behaviors that won't be tolerated—education in the virtues of care, steward-ship, and self-respect, regardless of whether such virtues fall neatly into the "fact" column on my worksheet? And wouldn't an education in such virtues—which so many teachers already unofficially work hard to encourage—demand the cultivation not only of my mind and critical faculties but of my whole being, including my emotions, my heart?

Such a program of education would require, of course, that "heart" be defined as more than *merely* the seat of emotions. We need not insist on a precise technical definition, but normal English usage in phrases such as "speaking from the heart" gives us a place to begin, with its implications of integrity and emotional warmth. What's not helpful is to separate too sharply (as we sometimes do) "head knowledge" and "heart knowledge." A more robust model is provided by the Hebrew tradition, according to which, as a person "thinketh in his heart, so he is" (Proverbs 23:7; KJV). In this tradition the heart encompasses the "three special functions [of] knowing, feeling, and willing." It is conceived as the "seat of the emotional and intellectual life," "of volition and of self-consciousness."[12] Again in the words of the Hebrew scriptures, "As water reflects the face, so one's life reflects the heart" (Proverbs 27:19; NIV).

A different but potentially complementary model of the human person derives from the ancient Greek philosopher Plato. Plato conceived of the embodied human soul as having a three-layered structure comprising the mind (or reason), the "spirited element" (sometimes interpreted as will), and the appetites (also passions or emotions).[13] In the well-ordered soul, the first of these informs and controls the second, and the second has the job of listening to the first and then governing the third. Or, in more familiar terms, the reason guides the will, which guides the emotions. In keeping with this model, a good education will strengthen and refine all three elements. It will involve not suppressing the emotions—which are recognized to be a powerful and legitimate component of the integrated human being—but shaping and regulating them.

This more-than-merely materialist prospect brings us again to the poverty of "facts vs. opinions" and an educational establishment too squeamish to promote actual virtues and the kind of integrity that most of us long for. In all these apparent efforts to educate, what place is left for "the supreme virtues of love, trust, hope, mercy, kindness, forgiveness and reconciliation"? Do those things really matter? If so, how is their importance conveyed to the children and students in our schools? Or do curricular materials such as those of the Common Core not instead simply convey the assumption, as two recent scholars have put it, "that most of reality has nothing to do with either good or evil, that it is just 'there' in its underived givenness,"[14] like a series of disembodied facts? But of course our children's curriculum implies that facts are highly important, even though in doing so it conveys a value judgment, which according to *it* must therefore be treated as merely an opinion! The incoherence could hardly be more radical, or more unhelpful and uninstructive for young people trying to make sense of their lives and of the world. There's nothing about such relegation of statements of value to the "opinion" column on their worksheets that fortifies students' spirits, strengthens their souls, encourages virtuous character, or awakens students (or any of us) "from the slumber of cold vulgarity."[15]

Three decades ago the American philosopher Alan Bloom framed what he called "the educational question of our times" as "Are we lovers anymore?"[16] More recently, proponents of virtue ethics have averred that "the ethical is a normal and essential ingredient of human action."[17] We need not adopt any one particular formulation to recognize how foreign such statements will sound to anyone schooled in Common-Core-style facts and opinions. For virtue-ethicists and their allies unashamedly address issues of good vs. evil, of virtue vs. vice, and treat these things as central, not peripheral, to education and to the world about which schools (we must still hope) aim to teach our children. Such issues pertain, *of course*, to the cultivation and integrity of the whole person, encompassing reason *and* will *and* emotion.

This triple emphasis is essential. According to the classical view, in the well-governed *psyche,* reason contributes crucially to how we discern right and wrong and how we actually practice morality. But one still-influential legacy of the eighteenth-century Enlightenment is a constricted view of reason as passive rationality: a kind of calculator that serves the will and the emotions rather than actively shaping and guiding them. Perhaps most notoriously, the Scottish philosopher David Hume declared that "Reason is, and ought only to be the slave of the passions," and moreover that "'Tis not contrary to reason to prefer the destruction of the whole world to the scratching of my finger."[18] Even the "reasoned judgment" called for in the Core Curriculum's "Reading Standards for Literacy" sounds more promising than that.

A further crucial question we need to consider here is whether what human beings know, love, and value is *merely* a subjective projection or a social "construction." We can accept that culture, language, and biology play major roles in our understanding of virtue, right, wrong, justice, injustice, and so on. But does this deny the possibility of a reality in some sense "out there" that is not purely relative to our individual or collective whims and subjectivities? Until the present epoch, most educators (among others) "believed the universe to be such that certain emotional reactions on our part could be either congruous or incongruous to it ... that objects did not merely receive, but could *merit*, our approval or disapproval, our reverence, or our contempt."[19] In this view, such acts of judgment are not mainly "about us," but instead refer ultimately to "something beyond ... that we do not measure and define, but by which we are measured and defined."[20]

The early Christian writer Augustine of Hippo wrote that the "true definition of virtue" can be given as "the order of love" (*ordo amoris*). "We do well to love that which, when we love it, makes us live well and virtuously."[21] Virtuous love is thus not just a subjective or arbitrary projection but a response to a good that is truly *there*, one that shapes us more than we shape it. In seventeenth-century England, Thomas Traherne asked, "Can you ... be

19

Righteous, unless you be just in rendering to Things their due esteem? All things were made to be yours; and you were made to prize them according to their value."[22] Again, the value of "Things" is no mere projection, and our esteem of their qualities is not "just an opinion."

This view of learning, with its "realism" regarding things in the world, goes back to ancient times. Aristotle, citing his own teacher Plato, says that "what a good education means" is "having been definitely trained from childhood to like and dislike the proper things." Therefore, "in order to be a competent student of the Right and Just ... the pupil is bound to have been well-trained in his habits. For the starting-point or first principle is the fact that a thing is so."[23] Once more, the assumption is that "the Right and Just" are in a profound sense there in the fabric of reality—that they are *so*—and that we humans don't invent them but instead must attune ourselves to them.

Such realism regarding "the Right and Just" is by no means limited only to classical and Christian thought. As Roy Rappaport has pointed out, there are concepts virtually identical with each other in ancient Egyptian, Iranian (Zoroastrian), and Vedic (Hindu) traditions: respectively, *Ma'at*, *Asha*, and *Rta*, each of which can be glossed as "cosmic law or order," "right," or "truth."[24] Rappaport calls these concepts "Ultimate Sacred Postulates," and they form unchanging foundations upon which communities and cultures can themselves change and evolve.

Moreover, he acknowledges the role, already mentioned, of the Enlightenment in inverting the status of ultimate postulates: In the legacy of the Enlightenment, "you have your opinion; I have mine. Ultimate knowledge, regnant knowledge is knowledge of fact. ... And what had been ultimate knowledge is now mere belief and what had been highly sanctified values are now reduced to the status of mere preferences."[25] This Enlightenment pattern has the ring of familiarity for anyone acquainted with curricula that our schools are required to teach children today.

Not surprisingly, cultures that affirm the *Rta* build their educational philosophies upon it instead. The Hindu, Buddhist, and Sikh concept of Dharma entails the individual's and society's duty to align themselves with that ultimate postulate or cosmic law. The qualities of "Truth, Love, Beauty, Goodness, Bliss and Consciousness" therefore "represent the spiritual values of a human being that are realized walking the path of righteousness."[26] This concept of a "path" or "road" in turn leads us to the great Chinese, Confucian, and Taoist philosophy of the Way, the *Tao*: "the primordial source of order and the guarantor of the stability of all appearance ... the unproduced Producer of all that is." And like *Ma'at*, *Asha*, and *Rta*—as well as like the Law, the Torah, of Jewish and biblical tradition—the *Tao* is a "teaching" and "the way humans should follow." "To live in accord with Tao is to realize [its] order and nature and stability in one's own life and society."[27]

Following C. S. Lewis, I will use "the *Tao*" as a rough shorthand for the array of ultimate postulates mentioned so far. Definitions of these vary across different cultures (though not as radically as is sometimes presumed), and it is only wise to concede that human knowledge of ultimate things is fallible and "situated." But what they all have in common is the profound sense that they are real, true, and foundational for the exercise of morality. The *Tao* thus understood might therefore help rescue our pale modern vocabulary of "appropriate" and "inappropriate" from the domain of mere jargon. For in contemplating the *Tao*, we realize that some attitudes and behaviors are indeed appropriate or inappropriate—fitting or unfitting, harmonious or dissonant—relative to something immensely greater and less transient than our own socially or individually constructed codes and opinions.

Norms, according to this view, are therefore understood as truly foundational rather than just conventional. And so the *Tao* permits us to rise above mere emotion or instinct or biology, and above simple family, social, or cultural convention. For example, for reasons connected with upbringing or individual disposition or even "evolutionary psychology," one may feel uncomfortable around people who are elderly or very young or less healthy, or even "foreign" in some way, and so avoid contact with them. However, from within the *Tao*, one recognizes that one's avoidance of human beings who are thus "different" from oneself is actually a moral shortcoming. At a deep level, it is not *reasonable*. Despite one's gut or emotional or even "instinctive" reactions to such people, one *should not* merely give in to one's tendency to turn away from them.

Yet according to curricula propagated and taught in today's schools, sentences expressing norms, values, "shoulds," and "oughts" fall into the dubious domain of mere opinion, and the moral "roadwork" of the *Tao* is thus eroded and undermined. I have no doubt that in practice most educators are better than their principles. The curricular materials mentioned earlier, however, cannot but vitiate teachers' noble efforts to cultivate virtuous people and good citizens. Unless we speak from within the *Tao*, our own virtues and appeals to virtue will inevitably appear arbitrary and lacking a proper foundation in any ultimate postulate, in any *Reason* worthy of the name.

How then can our society hope for cultural, moral, and political leaders of integrity and high principle if we continue to teach young people and ourselves that value judgments constitute purely subjective and probably self-serving opinions? Or that Reason is a mere calculator of data and an organ, at best, of "critical thinking"? Or that human emotions simply "are what they are"? Where are the places in our curricula and schools for the making of souls and the fortifying of hearts? The medieval philosopher Alain of Lille wrote that "In the heart, as in the midst of the human city, magnanimity has established her dwelling-place, and, acknowledging her service under the dominion of wisdom, works as that authority determines."[28] The heart—magnanimity (literally, greatness of soul)—governed by wisdom and in turn governing the emotions: Is this not what our children need, what we *all* need, more than carefully framed but morally ineffectual codes of conduct specifying "challenging" behaviors?

Instead, we today continue to propagate curricula and teaching materials that place us and our children outside the *Tao*, squeamish about ultimate postulates and embarrassed to speak of virtues or paths of righteousness. And so we are left flailing in our attempts to justify what behaviors and educational goals are appropriate or not. We somehow do not see the contradiction of producing cynics while expecting idealists. The idealism and integrity we all hope for surely require, instead of externally imposed codes and guidelines, a harmonious connection between the well nurtured core of the individual and a reality that transcends mere biology or social convention. We certainly need to go beyond any view according to which (in the words of George Grant) "human beings are really just lumps of matter."[29] If we desire to raise a generation of citizens prepared to embody wisdom, magnanimity, courage, character, virtue, then in our schools and in our teaching we must begin by forswearing the cultivation of humans without hearts.

2

The Way

Any education founded on the proposition that all judgments of value—all "oughts," all standards of morality—
are ultimately just subjective opinions must collapse into
incoherence. And it will surely threaten with a similar fate
any society built on such teaching. Of course, for anyone
who stands within the *Tao*, that prospect of collapse does
not by itself entail a refutation of subjectivism or relativism, for such a person will pursue truth (if it *is* truth) even
unto death. It would indeed be foolish to ignore the danger; but danger alone is no disproof. Yet there are deeper
reasons for us to be skeptical of moral relativism—regardless of whether moral judgments are declared to be
relative to biology, relative to an individual, or relative to
a whole culture.

By declaring that values are relative to each individual, or relative to a particular culture (whether broadly
or narrowly conceived), or relative to some evolutionary
contingency, educators who teach subjectivism and moral

relativism may honestly aim to enrich and to protect, rather than to corrupt, the minds of their students. They may quite rightly wish to cultivate virtues of open-mindedness and tolerance. And no doubt they do so in opposition to the *in*tolerance—dogmat*ism*, moral*ism*—of which history provides so many horrific examples.

It is important to remember, however, that open-mindedness and tolerance are secondary or "instrumental" virtues—pursued not so much for their own sake as for the sake of the more foundational virtues in which they are rooted. Open-mindedness is good because it encourages us to be humble, and to consider the thoughts and needs, even the worth and the humanity, of others. It thus promotes (while not guaranteeing) harmony, peace, respect, and civil conversation. Tolerance likewise promotes peace among people, and among groups of people. So, upon reflection, anyone can see that these virtues are limited, not ultimate. Open-mindedness stops short of acquiescence to honor-killings or racism, for example. As for tolerance, similarly, it is clearly a virtue—until it is not. Innumerable codes of conduct across varying school systems—as well as in government, law, health care, and so on—today declare unapologetically that harassment, bullying, vandalism, violence, possession of illicit drugs, and the like "will not be tolerated."

Well and good. But the problem is that teaching-materials in those same school systems offer scant wisdom that might help young people or educators discern where the line should be drawn between virtuous tolerance and a principled refusal to tolerate. As we've already noticed, the prevalent simple-minded distinction between facts and opinions—today taught almost everywhere—renders schools' codes of conduct *arbitrary* rather than principled. For example, according to one typical Common Core worksheet used for teaching twelve-year-olds, the statements "Copying homework assignments is wrong" and "Cursing in school is inappropriate behavior" are just opinions. And if that is correct, then surely any claim that "bullying is wrong" or "vandalism is immoral" must likewise fall into the same dubious and unreliable category. Thus, a deep fault line runs between what schools claim to be—with the goods and "shoulds" that are their very reason for being—and the lessons they actually teach about value, virtue, and purpose.

We noticed already in Chapter 1 how schools and departments of education often cloak their professed "goods and shoulds" in language that obscures the moral judgments any human being or any human institution fundamentally accepts as not merely subjective but instead objectively valid and real. Smashing school furniture and head banging are accordingly identified as "challenging behaviors" that the school's administration does not approve of and will not tolerate. Such actions may furthermore be declared "negative" or "inappropriate" or not in keeping with "expectations."

But *why* are such behaviors not to be tolerated? If you stand within the *Tao*, if you affirm the reality of a moral foundation, of the existence of ultimate sacred postulates, then you will say—if you're bold enough—that those intolerable behaviors are fundamentally wrong. Yet for anyone *not* standing within the *Tao*, the answer to that question is reducible to an arbitrary "just because," or "because we (the administration) say so—and if you cross us, we have ways of making you regret it"—or to some other relativistic appeal to "that's how things are in this system, and you'll be expelled if you don't play by our rules." In short, in the absence of a solid sense of *right*, there is no recourse except to a strong sense of *might*.[30]

It is not as if educators who frame codes of conduct and statements of purpose don't have a clear notion of what is right and good. The very fact that they identify the *purpose* of their schools indicates that they aim at something they consider good and truly desirable. In fact, all such statements reveal what philosophers might call a powerful sense of "teleology"—from Greek *telos*, "end," or "purpose."

Indeed, human beings seem to be creatures persistently in search of purpose, even if at times that purpose may elude us. We try to plan our lives, our projects, our futures, and yes our schools in a way that pursues a purpose:

some goal or condition or action that we believe is right and good. Of course, we may pursue things that end up proving to be "false goods" because they're actually only transitory, or too narrowly or selfishly defined, or simply illusory. But the very fact that schools and departments of education have statements of purpose shows decisively that they participate in this universal if fallible human drive to pursue the good. This is the drive behind statements such as the Ontario Education Ministry's Code of Conduct, which declares that a school "should be a place that promotes responsibility, respect, civility, and academic excellence." Again, who could object to such aims?

My objection, however, is not against such commendably teleological language. It is against the relativizing and subjectivizing philosophy that explicitly or implicitly pervades the actual curriculum in those schools—and that therefore corrodes in the classroom the principles proclaimed over the school's front door or on its homepage.

The very statement of those principles reveals the wish to pursue *something* not itself susceptible to the acid of relativism or subjectivism. Even if a statement of purpose is couched in language about activities, practices, or behaviors that are "necessary," ultimately those who speak this language must answer the questions "necessary for what?" An honest reply will reveal that they do have a purpose or end-point they consider good for its own sake—and not merely good in a way that can then be dismissed as "just your opinion." We can perform the same critical analysis on any claim that somebody's attitudes, desires, educational philosophy, politics and so on are "progressive" or modern. These terms remain mere "vacuous self-congratulation"[31] unless there's a coherent answer to the question "progress toward what substantively good state of affairs?" or "modern in what truly beneficial sense?"

One crucial test of a system of moral thought is presented by the issue of death for a good cause. As already indicated, for someone who stands squarely within the *Tao*, there are certain things for which he or she should be willing to die. To narrow the focus, let's assume that, morally, there are circumstances in which it is right and good for me to die for my country, or my family, or my friend, or even for an endangered stranger. I admit that this is not a comfortable topic. My first response to it is to ask, "Are there *any* circumstances in which I would have the heart, the courage (a word deriving from the concept of heart), to sacrifice my life for that of another?" But of course the prior moral question here is not "would I?" but "should I?"

One reason for a "yes" to the latter question is offered by Jesus' words in the gospels: "Greater love has no one than this: to lay down one's life for one's friends" (John

15:13; NIV). The good that underlies the "should" is thus closely connected with "*agápē*," the Greek word for a love virtually defined by self-sacrifice and exemplified by that willingness to die: to give up everything you know and enjoy about this present life for the sake of someone else. The "good" achieved by such a death is therefore by the nature of the case an ultimate or "transcendent" good; it can't possibly be a good that the self-sacrificing individual acquires or enjoys immanently, in this life—for such a person is now dead. And yet those who stand within the *Tao*, whose moral thought and life are grounded in the ultimate sacred postulates, will say of the self-sacrificial hero, "Yes, she did the right thing." Certainly as nations and societies, we affirm that judgment when we celebrate the self-giving heroism of soldiers, police, firefighters, or other brave citizens who have died serving their fellow human beings. In the words of Seneca the Roman, "Praise and imitate the one who, though he loves life, is not grieved to die."

But what about those who seek to ground morality in something other than the *Tao*—perhaps in Enlightened Reason, or a philosophy of utilitarianism, or cultural norms, or biology, or evolutionary psychology, or a school curriculum that teaches children that "shoulds and goods" are matters of subjective opinion? Can any such approach offer an adequate justification for the sentiments and judgments we express when we laud fallen heroes?

As we noticed in Chapter 1, the Enlightenment developed a definition of reason that tended to strip it of its practical or moral role. Asking Enlightenment reason "What should I do in such and such circumstances?" will be met with the answer "It depends what you desire." For Enlightenment reason functions only as a kind of computer that performs cost-benefit-analysis but relies on someone else or something else to specify the good that is to be sought. Again to cite David Hume, "Reason is, and ought only to be the slave of the passions." Reason's job is accordingly to *calculate* whether it's less desirable to have one's finger scratched or to envisage the destruction of the whole world.

This narrow species of reason accordingly offers no practical guidance unless an "I desire" or an "I ought" is imported from something that is itself not reason. It should be conceded that Hume believed in the existence and legitimacy of "moral sentiments," so he doesn't necessarily fall in with the kind of relativists who later aimed to "debunk" sentiments altogether. Nonetheless, as Hume so starkly showed, driving a wedge between reason and sentiment is one definite step toward an impoverished "fact-vs.-opinion" carving up of the world.

The other obvious problem with sentiment-divorced-from-reason as a guide to morality it that it can dictate contrary things. If you observe me pondering whether to sacrifice my life to save someone else's, *your* moral sentiments might be cheering me on while *mine* are quailing and hesitant. Unless my sentiments are guided by a *Tao*-informed reason and a trained will (as sketched in Chapter 1), they may prove weak and fickle indeed. Faced with the prospect of my own self-sacrifice, no matter how noble you and the other spectators say it is, I may just not *feel* like it.

But what if we move from Enlightenment reason to utilitarianism—an ethical theory according to which "good" is defined in terms of the greatest usefulness to the greatest number of people? The self-sacrificial death now gets analyzed in terms of its usefulness to the wider community. As Lewis points out, in such a calculus, only the death of *some* of its members can be said to be useful to the community as a whole; it would be nonsense to say that the death of the whole community could be useful to the community.[32] Thus, to the extent that this approach recommends anyone's self-sacrificial death, it urges some members to die for the sake of the survival of other members. Yet even if it can demonstrate, for example, that your death will result in others' survival (a utilitarian "good"), it seems impotent (without recourse to non-utilitarian appeals to love or honor) to convince you that *you* ought to be the one to risk your life.

You might quite understandably demand a reason *why* you should perform the recommended act of heroism and self-sacrifice. And if the person so recommending understands "reason" only in the Enlightenment sense—as a series of calculations applied to an established set of empirical facts—then he or she will be reduced to the familiar contortions of someone hopelessly trying to extract an "ought" from an "is." If you *refuse* the recommended act of self-sacrifice intended to preserve the life of another, or even the lives of a whole community, you are not acting irrationally in that narrow Enlightenment sense of "reason." The claim "Your self-sacrifice will save the lives of others" does not imply "You *ought* to sacrifice your life for the preservation of others"—unless we add the premise that the lives of your fellow human beings *ought* to be preserved. Again, on the Enlightenment model, no "ought" may logically appear in the conclusion of the argument unless there's already an "ought" in the premises.

Put in a different way, unless you stand within the *Tao* and so already have a strong sense of obligation and duty—unless you possess a set of virtues that infuse not only your reason (in the rich sense of *practical* reason, or judgment) but also your will and emotions—you may remain unmoved by the persuasions of those urging that only through your self-sacrifice will others' lives be preserved. Yet if you do possess that sense of duty and recognition of obligation to preserve your community, these do of course involve your sentiments or emotions but are no "*mere* sentiments but are rationality itself."[33] By contrast, those wishing to replace the *Tao* with something

34

else, some other ground of obligation—something less ultimate, less transcendent—give up looking for a truly rational core for morality or virtue and hunt instead for a foundation that they think is more realistic, or somehow more basic.

❧

Those seeking that foundational "something else" often turn to the domain of biology, whether by means of an extended account of evolutionary psychology or, in somewhat less sophisticated language, with recourse to "instinct." If, as seems to be the case, genes and species naturally seek to replicate themselves, then surely the "value" of preserving society is just an extension of those instinctive individual and collective urges.

But even this superficially plausible formulation reveals weaknesses inherent in any exclusive appeal to instinct or to "urges." My urges, your urges, and the collective urges of an institution or wider society to which we both belong might all drive in contrary directions. To return to the unpleasant "challenging" school behaviors cited earlier—vandalism, stealing, bullying, and the like—it might be quite easy to explain them as arising from a given individual's urges and instincts. And if the school principal felt in turn the instinctive urge to expel the transgressing student, that too would not strike anyone as inexplicable. However, the collective judgment of the school's administration as a whole might reveal yet other instincts, namely more moderate desires to keep the peace and to mete out punishment without jeopardizing the student's educational progress. Or is this collective urge *only* an instinct? Isn't it something more?

The point that can be inferred from any such scenario is that the morally best course of action is chosen on the basis *not* of instinct alone but of some reasonable principle transcending instinct and not merely reducible to it. Put in another way, when the dictates of various instincts clash, it is not simply yet another instinct that casts a deciding vote about which one is to be obeyed. To defend an action with "I did it instinctively" might not be completely irrelevant when all things are considered. But in a court of law, much else would indeed be considered, and the explanation from instinct would not trump other reasons for the verdict that a certain deed should be either condemned or excused. In short, instinct alone is an insufficient ground for moral judgment.

Both history and reason warn us, of course, that appeals to instinct or to large-scale supposedly biological urges often serve to justify downright *immoral* behavior on the part of people or groups of people making those appeals. Fascist or racist ideologies, for example, may appeal to evolution, or to the survival of the fittest, or to some account of one's membership in a master race. Or a hard-core communist ideology may appeal to the inevitable victory of a particular social or economic class to justify communism's own atrocities. Such ideologies may support what appears to be a new set of sexual, familial, civic, and interpersonal morals. But upon inspection these are mere parodies of morality, or scraps of morality wrenched from the *Tao* (if they are even that), while the wider and deeper foundation is abandoned. In such cases, the much-vaunted "preservation of the species" is turned in fact into the preservation of part of the species at the expense of the destruction of other parts of it.

I am not here making a case against taking instinct, or biology, or evolutionary psychology seriously in an overall account of human behavior or morality. This is emphatically not an argument suggesting that we should ignore or suppress the lessons of genuine science. It *is* an argument against treating those things as, by themselves, sufficient grounds for the human consideration of right and wrong.

Probably the most influential evolutionary biologist of all time apart from Charles Darwin himself was T. H. Huxley (1825-1895), popularly known as "Darwin's Bulldog." Huxley, who in matters pertaining to religion was an avowed *agnostic* (a term he himself coined), nonetheless saw very clearly the insufficiency of evolution alone as a foundation of morals. In a lecture on "Evolution and Ethics" delivered late in his career,[34] Huxley reviews various characteristics that he sees as accounting for humankind's "success in the struggle for existence": "self-assertion, the unscrupulous seizing upon all that can be grasped, the tenacious holding of all that can be kept"; in short, "qualities which [humankind] shares with the ape and the tiger; … cunning … sociability … curiosity" as well as "ruthless and ferocious destructiveness." However, in what Huxley sees as our now more advanced state, "civilized man brands all these ape and tiger promptings with the name of sins," and "there is a general consensus that the ape and tiger methods of the struggle for existence are not reconcilable with sound ethical principles."

This contrast between the workings of biology and the norms of human ethics appears starkly in specific cases within the animal kingdom. Recent research into the social and reproductive practices of geladas—large baboon-like monkeys inhabiting the mountains of Ethiopia—offers a case in point. Geladas live in units of a single dominant male and up to a dozen females. But bachelor groups threaten and sometimes oust that dominant male. When this happens, a new dominant male gains reproductive access to the group's females and kills perhaps half of all his predecessor's offspring, while 80% of female geladas pregnant at the time of the ousting soon abort the fetuses they are carrying.[35] A similar male practice of infanticide also occurs among African lions. And be it among geladas, lions, or other species, such infanticide serves not only to diminish the genetic legacy of the newly dominant male's predecessor, but also to accelerate the fertility of the females (which cease to lactate and thus resume ovulation) so that the new, infanticidal alpha male can establish *his* genetic legacy as quickly as possible.

Those hoping to infer principles of morality from natural history often appeal to "positive" behaviors such as altruism that appear in various animal species. However, more shocking behaviors such as lions' and geladas' infanticide make such inferences problematic. Do we look to some still higher instinct that will help us adjudicate which lower instincts to obey—altruism or infanticide— or perhaps which behaviors humans themselves should emulate? Again the point is not that animal behaviors have no relevance to our understanding of human behavior, but rather that we require a standard of judgment above and beyond that offered by bare biology as a guide to what is morally permissible, advantageous, or obligatory.[36]

Zoologists studying animal behavior don't of course either approve or disapprove of infanticide among geladas or lions. In the words of the common cliché, it is what it is. But when we turn our attention to human behavior, we do express approval or disapproval, satisfaction or disappointment, affirmative or negative judgment. Huxley sees this response as involving something of a paradox, given his convictions about human origins out of what he calls "the cosmic process." At some point in this process "the conscience of man revolted against the moral indifference

of nature, and the microcosmic atom [we humans!] …
found the illimitable macrocosm guilty." Thus there is a
sharp clash between the "is" of nature and the "ought" that
we apply to human beings. And given such a clash, it again
seems futile to regard that "ought" as something merely
arising from the empirical "is." For as Huxley observes,
"cosmic nature is no school of virtue."

So once more it appears that biology, instinct, and
appeals to evolutionary science fall short of offering an
adequate conception of right and wrong. Whatever "is"
they point to offers no reliable foundation for "ought."
Huxley also points back to Alexander Pope's pre-Darwin-
ian, Enlightenment argument—or rather, assertion—that
"whatever is is right" (*The Essay on Man*; 1733). Accusing
the poet of "mere cheap rhetoric," Huxley punctures
Pope's and others' attempts to derive morality ("right")
from "whatever is." He points out how such philosophical
"optimism" (the teaching that this world is *optimus*, "the
best") leaves humankind—morally—"with every aspira-
tion stifled and every effort paralyzed." For "Why try to set
right what is already right? Why strive to improve the best
of all possible worlds?"[37] As Lewis comments, referring
to educators' promotion of moral improvement among
their students, "Why this stream of exhortation to drive
us where we cannot help going? Why such praise for those
who have submitted to the inevitable?"[38]

Despite how interesting biology may be for the human study of right and wrong, therefore, Huxley argues that evolution "is incompetent to furnish any [adequate] reason why what we call good is preferable to what we call evil." He recognizes that some may be tempted to see evolutionary development itself in quasi-moral terms, for it can appear that certain species including our own have over time "advanced," or "improved," or "progressed" to higher states. But this, Huxley suggests, is a fallacy that "has arisen out of the unfortunate ambiguity of the phrase 'survival of the fittest.' 'Fittest' has a connotation of 'best'; and about 'best' there hangs a moral flavour."

Properly speaking, however, "fitness" has to do with an organism's adaptation to its environment, so that, for example, should the climate of the northern hemisphere cool, "the survival of the fittest might bring about, in the vegetable kingdom, a population of more and more stunted and humbler and humbler organisms, until the 'fittest' that survived might be nothing but lichens, diatoms, and … microscopic organisms." So much for evolutionary "advancement" or "progress"! And thus even Huxley, foremost agnostic and evolutionist of his age, concludes that "the cosmic process has no sort of relation to moral ends," indeed that "the ethical progress of society depends, not on imitating the cosmic process, … but in combating it."

∽

If such things as evolution, biology more generally, and instinct alone do not determine "moral ends" or the shape of "ethical progress," then what does? The other currently dominant attempt to ground standards of right and wrong emerges not from the science of biology but broadly from anthropology and sociology. Instead of seeing morals as arising from a biologically shaped population that emerges from Huxley's evolutionary "cosmic process," many in the so-called human sciences regard morals as products of a particular culture or society. In slightly different language: right and wrong are socially, culturally, or linguistically "constructed." They are thus *relative* to their society, culture, or language of origin, and so ultimately incommensurable with standards constructed by another society, culture, or language. Given this frame for thought, "It is wrong for me to commit murder" translates to "Murder is disapproved of in my culture."

This view, often called "social constructionism," in effect declares that moral judgments are not "just your opinion" but instead "just *your society's or culture's* opinion." It is subjectivism raised from the level of the individual to that of the collective—but is subjectivism nonetheless. Social constructionism is an extrapolation from the obvious fact that when we look at different cultures, we notice striking differences in how things are done and what things are valued. We could make endless lists of variations in how people in different countries eat differently, speak differently, behave differently in traffic, have different expectations of their parents and of their children, are embarrassed by different personal questions, and so on.

One characteristic of human perception, however, is that we notice difference more readily than we do sameness, and this tendency can cause us to overlook what apparently disparate cultures truly do have in common. Many fundamental laws or moral tenets such as the preservation and solidarity of humanity in fact transcend cultural boundaries. Confucius teaches that for the noble person, for the gentleman, "everyone within the Four Seas is his brother."[39] The Stoic writes, "I am a man: I consider that nothing human is alien to me."[40] "Do to others as you would have them do to you," says Jesus (Luke 6:31; NIV). "By the fundamental law of nature," writes John Locke, "man [is] to be preserved as much as possible."[41] Such trans- or supra-cultural tenets do not by themselves *prove* the existence or validity of the *Tao*, although they do render its existence and validity more plausible. Nor do they alone *disprove* social constructionism. But they certainly pose a problem for the lazy assumption that standards of right and wrong are merely cultural or social constructs—and therefore that we, standing as each of us does within such a social/cultural/historical context, have no business forming judgments about the validity or coherence of the standards affirmed by people who live in another context. In short, it is illogical and unjustified to infer from differences among peoples and cultures that standards of right and wrong are likewise essentially or necessarily heterogeneous.

On the contrary, the truth of deep moral principles—ultimate sacred postulates—bears a strong analogy to the truth of mathematical axioms. They are true, but not because something else makes them true. Yes, mathematical truths (some of them) have great practical application outside mathematics: in physics, technology, engineering, everyday finance, and so on. But anyone demanding practical *empirical* proof of a basic mathematical claim doesn't understand the nature of mathematics. An axiom is either presupposed or self-evident, and valid mathematical theorems and corollaries are deduced from them by a rigorous chain of reasoning. The truth of 2+3=5, accordingly, does not depend on its being proved by my adding two apples to three apples and getting five apples. It is a *useful* piece of arithmetic, certainly; but it is not true *because* it is useful. Moreover, its truth transcends both biology and social convention; it is not true in one culture and false in another.[42] The truth of 2+3=5 is simply part of the deep structure of reality, regardless of whether any given culture recognizes it to be such.

It is perfectly imaginable, for example, that we might discover some culture somewhere that has no knowledge of Pythagoras's Theorem: "the square on the hypotenuse of a right angle triangle is equal to the sum of the squares on the other two sides." This theorem is not only capable of numerous mathematical proofs but is also highly useful in various practical pursuits such as construction, land surveying, and so on. And if we imagine further that a geometrician introduces it to the culture that was previously unaware of it, would she be censured for cultural condescension or mathematical imperialism? Surely not. For although mathematics may well be valued and expressed differently from society to society, we do not treat a theorem such as the Pythagorean one as *essentially* culturally constructed. Its introduction to a society that hadn't known about it before would accordingly be viewed as a benefit, not a mark of disrespect, even if the geometrician introducing it had to work hard to convince members of that society of its validity. Initially, of course, she might demonstrate in practice how the theorem works, how it is useful. But in the end, her job would be incomplete until she had shown people how the theorem follows necessarily from postulates.

The analogy between mathematical and moral postulates helps us to see (a) that ultimately mathematical truth must be grounded in mathematical principles, not in an appeal to the "facts" of physics, of history, or of a particular culture (even though it might prove useful in these domains); and (b) that moral truth must likewise be acknowledged to be grounded in moral principles—in foundational "oughts" and "shoulds"—that are not merely adventitious or culturally constructed.

The analogy furthermore suggests how moral progress might take place within a culture or society in a way that does not entail a change in, or an abandonment of, the moral postulates themselves—indeed, might spring up from them. In the society that we imagined as previously ignorant of Pythagoras's Theorem, it was not the case that the geometrical principles upon which the theorem is founded did not exist, only that either they had not yet been recognized or that their implications had not yet been discerned. Similarly, it may be that certain societies, even ones claiming to acknowledge the "axiom" of the Golden Rule expressed in Jesus' "Do to others as you would have them do to you," did not until recently (or perhaps have not yet) discerned what this principle entails, for example, for sexual and racial equality. But in this way, the *Tao*, although firm and profoundly unchanging, is the soil from which dynamic moral development can arise, and in which our individual and collective understandings can grow deeper and richer.

Before we leave this analogy, let's consider two important but potentially problematic words: "obvious" and "useful." "Obvious" can have a subjective dimension that might render it slippery. But most mathematicians agree that, once we thoroughly understand the terms of an arithmetical axiom or theorem, its truth is self-evident, or obvious—even if its more extended corollaries or implications might not be. Indeed, "obvious" as applied to axioms need not imply "easily grasped or arrived at." Yet if you insist on remaining skeptical about the assertion "if A = B, and B = C, then A = C," you will soon disqualify yourself from conversation with mathematicians. If you exercise persistent doubt about that assertion, or if you demand some "factual" proof of it from outside the domain of mathematics, it won't be long before your credibility is in tatters.

Likewise, if you challenge the moral and evaluative claims that "you ought to do to others as you would have them do to you," or that "genocide is wrong," or that a country in which people are healthy and secure is (other things being equal) better than one in which they are sick, hungry, and plagued by violence, then it appears you are either simply obtuse or else perverse, having cut yourself and your thinking off from the *Tao*. For those claims, though not true by definition, are obvious in the sense just defined. They are moral truths. If you demand that they be proved by criteria outside the realm of morality—or if you insist that they are merely matters of opinion—then you eventually exclude yourself from serious conversation concerning them. As Confucius teaches, "Do not take counsel with those who follow a different Way [*Tao*]."[43]

So it is that many, especially those working in the social sciences, undermine their credibility, occasionally even in their own eyes. In fact, some have reached the point where they can no longer live with the contradictions between the cultural relativism permeating their disciplines and the universals that they both recognize intellectually and, as human beings, feel in their hearts.

For present purposes, two witnesses to this tension must suffice. Yale sociologist Philip Gorski declares that "The social sciences have an ethics problem"; they exhibit "a failure … to develop a satisfactory theory of ethical life … that could explain why humans are constantly judging and evaluating … A theory that could explain something so trivial as the fact that social scientists care about data fudging." Gorski continues: It's not "that we have no theories. It's just that they're bad theories." And speaking as a social scientist himself, he recognizes that "we can't be complete relativists in our everyday lives. There is no escaping ethical life."[44]

Anthropologist Carolyn Fluehr-Lobban also found she could not escape this ethical imperative—and so courageously reassessed what had been her "relativist reflex to almost any challenge to cultural practice on moral or philosophical grounds." "For example, I would readily criticize rampant domestic violence in the U.S. and then attempt to rationalize the killing of wives and sisters from the Middle East to Latin America by men whose 'honor' had been violated by their female relations' alleged misdeeds, from flirtation to adultery." However, having rejected what she admits was a "double standard"—although at times "relativism may frame and enlighten the debate"—she now acknowledges that "in the end, moral judgment and human rights take precedence and choices must be made."[45] Fluehr-Lobban's impressive and honest conclusion was hard-won. And yet, once she has arrived at it, it seems obvious.

In this discussion, therefore, "obvious" does not imply that moral decisions are "easily arrived at" or that recognizing the *Tao* eliminates the hard work, sometimes even the agony, of moral discernment. Instead, it means that there's an "of course" that comes at the end, rather than at the beginning, of that process of discernment. Again, rather like the extended effort that goes into our grasping a mathematical truth deduced from axioms, the work demanded before we attain a moral realization can eventuate in the exclamation "Of course! That's obvious! How could I not have seen that before?" And likewise for Fluehr-Lobban's recognition that a transcultural condemnation of violence against women is the right stance to take: It emerges—although only after a determined struggle with cultural relativism—with a sense that it ought to have been obvious all along. Of course!

What, then, about the relationship between the moral and the "useful"? Let's be clear that neither with mathematics nor with morality is there any reason to diminish or deny their usefulness. But that usefulness is not what constitutes their ground or their principal justification. We have already encountered the approach to matters of right and wrong known as utilitarianism, one version of which is "consequentialism." This approach assesses the morality of human actions according to whether they produce beneficial results. It has the attraction of sounding like good common sense, and some forms of it seek to place that assessment on a scientific or even universal foundation, one intended to escape the paralysis of cultural and ethical relativism.[46]

What is potentially "scientific" about utilitarianism, however, is the measurement of happiness created by allegedly good behaviors, actions, policies, rules and so on. Nor will adherents of the *Tao* object to such attempts at enhancing our understanding of the nature of happiness and of human flourishing. What they will object to is merely the pretense that the "oughts" of right and wrong can be exhaustively reduced to or derived from the "is" of a pragmatic yardstick. Pragmatic yardsticks can themselves undeniably be useful; but criteria such as "flourishing" can conceal assumptions about truth and goodness—about things that are actually prior to, and that transcend, the operation of any supposedly scientific measurement.[47] Utilitarianism and consequentialism, despite their commendable efforts to escape the paralysis of both individual subjectivism and social constructionism (itself, as already noted, a higher-order subjectivism), therefore cannot escape the charge that they impose a values-relativism of their own, one that is tied to the tools they use and to the hidden moral and cultural assumptions they employ.

So let usefulness be explored and celebrated! But our children and young people—all of us—in order to grow and flourish as moral, virtuous human beings, need more than utilitarian calculations. We need to rediscover the rich soil of the *Tao* and to acquire the deep motivations, the more-than-pragmatic sense of reason, of obligation, of virtue, of good judgment, and of the wholesome habits that its rediscovery can nurture and sustain.

3

Humanity Reclaimed

When "reason" is reduced to the status of a calculator that simply works in the service of fulfilling desires—be they political or economic, social or individual—human beings themselves become objects of manipulation by other human beings, by those with greatest power over the definition of what shall be considered reasonable, or even human. But by adhering to a richer notion of reason and of human dignity and integrity, one rooted in the *Tao*, we may offer our children and ourselves a clearer, more authentic, and more dynamic foundation for moral life, virtuous life. Such an approach continues to prize the achievements of science without the pitfalls of treating science as a mechanism for reducing human beliefs, values, and morals to "merely" the level of physical, psychological, or cultural phenomena. To glimpse the reality of the *Tao* is to gain new insight into moral first principles, and into the true glory of being human.

In trying to think reasonably and clearly about issues of right and wrong, however, we face a great challenge posed by quite contrary meanings of "nature." On the one hand, in appealing to the *Tao* as the source or foundation of moral judgment—as the repository of ultimate sacred postulates—we may treat it as Nature with a capital "N." The great Roman thinker Cicero wrote that "we ought to follow Nature as our guide, to contribute to the general good by an interchange of acts of kindness, by giving and receiving, and thus by our skill, our industry, and our talents to cement human society more closely together."[48] In the classical tradition, "Nature" can thus serve as a close synonym of the *Tao*. This sense of "Nature" continued to prevail through to the Middle Ages and beyond. It—or "she," the goddess *Natura*—was often invoked as a personified force, as in our still-current phrase "Mother Nature." Nature accordingly sometimes appears as equivalent to "Creation," or even as a power that shapes or guides creation and holds it together, something with inherent purpose, something essentially good.

And yet, as indicated in the last chapter, nature may also be treated merely as "the way things are"—as the "is" from which no "ought" can be derived. T. H. Huxley, as we have seen, speaks of "the moral indifference of nature" and declares that "cosmic nature is no school of virtue." Nature in this sense—and it's the word's dominant meaning in present-day scientific discussions—does not generally carry with it the assumption of divinity or purpose.[49] Modern science often operates within the framework of "methodological naturalism," that is, within the assumption that only investigations of nature alone (in this second sense), without any appeal to divinity or purpose ("teleology"), qualify as proper science. And science so conducted has undeniably produced a plenitude of fruitful results.

It can be a fine line, however, between naturalism as a methodology and naturalism as an all-encompassing view of the world. Although philosophers (being philosophers) distinguish and debate various forms of naturalism, for our purposes we can simply say that naturalism is a way of conceiving and engaging the world whereby nature is not only "the way things are" but also "all there is." And therefore what might sometimes seem to be behind or beyond or above or below nature must itself be reduced to, or explained in terms of, just nature. Nobody any more explains lightning in terms of the wrath of Zeus. We've learned instead that it's a phenomenon resulting when powerful charges of electricity discharge from, or between, clouds.

But things are not always that cut and dried. What happens when we apply methodological naturalism to much larger questions concerning all of human life or even the whole universe? Nobel-prize-winning physicist Steven Weinberg wrote, near the end of his famous book on cosmology, that "The more the universe seems comprehensible, the more it also seems pointless."[50] And in a way it's not surprising that a rigorously physics-based study of the cosmos might end with the conclusion that there's nothing behind or beyond or above or below it. That's how methodological naturalism proceeds, and so the innocent-looking naturalism present at the start of the argument emerges at the end as a thoroughgoing *philosophical* naturalism.[51]

Philosophical naturalism, however, as we've seen in previous chapters, demands a search for something social, psychological, biological, physical, or the like that underlies principles of right and wrong. In other words, it treats moral principles not truly *as* principles: for *principles* are things that by definition come *first*, that are foundational, that do indeed stand behind or beyond or above or below the contingencies of human behavior and that guide the decisions and judgments we make concerning them. Naturalism, by contrast, drives us to explain morality—virtue, standards of right and wrong, "oughts"—in terms of something it imagines is even more basic, by which it means more physical, more "natural" (*physis* being the Greek word for nature). Despite Huxley's assertion concerning the "moral indifference of nature," today's so-called social sciences in particular see morality as relative either to nature (instinct, biology, evolutionary psychology, etc.) or to "culture" or "society" naturalistically conceived. The problem here is that the more thoroughly the naturalistic social sciences explain such parts or manifestations of nature, the more these (like Weinberg's universe) seem ultimately pointless. For if value, purpose, teleology, and a substantial "ought" are banished from your premises and assumptions, then inevitably those things are also absent from your conclusions about life, humanity, and the world—and likewise inevitably from the education you offer your children.

Someone might of course reply, "Well, so much the worse for moral realism. Too bad for the *Tao*. It's not supported by science!" But of course this "lack of scientific support" arises from *premises* that are methodologically naturalistic. It is not something that legitimately emerges from evidence and a careful chain of reasoning. It is not a logical or empirical *conclusion*. Or, if it is a conclusion at all, it's one following from presuppositions that guarantee an absence of moral purpose in the "findings" of any science guided exclusively by those presuppositions. And yet, to defend moral realism against methodological naturalism is *not* to dismiss or denigrate science or scientists. It is simply to discern as carefully as we can the assumptions upon which science proceeds—and so also to discern what actually does or does not constitute a legitimate scientific conclusion.

There is a logical principle at work here that needs to be asserted. We might put it like this: *Mutual repugnance cuts both ways.*

If practitioners of methodological naturalism cast doubt on moral realism, failing to find, or to account for, purpose in the universe or in human society—and so conclude "too bad for the *Tao*"—then it is only fair to tell them that they are not exempt from the logic or implications of their own position. If naturalistic science cannot discern or explain purpose in the world or in our collective or individual lives, then that inability in turn implies "too bad for naturalism." For you and I and everybody else, including physicists and anthropologists, do have aims and goals. The very fabric of our lives is teleological—purpose-driven—in ways that far transcend the dissemination of our genes (though perhaps that's part of it). Therefore, a failure to account for that strong sense and experience of purpose, of goal-directedness, of moral worthwhileness, is a serious failure indeed. It points decisively to a *limitation* of science as naturalistically conceived and practiced.[52]

Yet this observation, let it be emphasized, is in no way an attack upon science, nor a devaluation of scientists or of scientific achievement. Rather, it is simply a sober acknowledgment of the existence of truths and domains that, for science-as-naturalistically-practiced, fall outside its sole jurisdiction. To echo Hamlet, "there are more things in heaven and earth" than are encompassed by the empirical method. That observation does of course imply a critique of what is sometimes called scient*ism*—essentially the assertion or assumption (not itself a scientific conclusion) that the scientific method is the adequate, all-encompassing, and sole arbiter of truth and human knowledge. But to warn against such overreaching is not to take a position hostile to genuine science nor toward its practitioners and their manifold attainments.

So the inability of naturalistic science to account for the "goods and shoulds" of human moral life might accordingly be treated less as a failure than as a blameless omission—a mere innocent incapacity to achieve something that was never part of its competence or job description in the first place.

But an acceptance of this account solves only part of our problem. We may "hear" the silence of science concerning ultimate moral foundations (though not necessarily concerning the practical "how to" of moral behavior) and then rush to the conclusion that "goods and shoulds" must merely be non-factual matters of opinion, and that disputes about moral right and wrong are unresolvable because each of us, and each of our respective cultures, simply view the world differently from one another. Of course it's not empirical science itself that's to blame for this apparent vacuum within our social and educational philosophy. Instead, what's at fault is the assumption that if empirical science doesn't produce reliable moral knowledge, then nothing else can.

Such is the thinking, or lack of thinking, that leads to the relegation of moral statements to the "opinion" column on worksheets aimed at helping students in our schools to separate fact from opinion. As argued in Chapter 1, such aspects of common educational curricula are incoherent as well as potentially damaging to students and in turn to our society. In particular, if we routinely teach students that statements containing words like "should" or "ought" or "good" are just opinions without factual content, then we undercut (among other things) the very norms, ideals, and purposes that motivate us to operate schools—to educate our children and ourselves—in the first place.

It's worth examining further how educational authorities struggle to fill the vacuum created by weak or nonexistent philosophical foundations. Many educators, administrators, and politicians evidently feel embarrassed by appeals to broadly human "goods" and virtues that (in our hearts) we hope to instill in our children. We've already noticed how school documents and codes habitually suppress the moral vocabulary of "good," "just," "decent," "virtuous" and so on, replacing it with pallid jargon such as "positive," "appropriate," and "expected." The lack of ethical robustness in this shift is even more apparent when we consider the terms' antonyms. To call bad behavior "evil," "unjust," "indecent," or "vicious" is truly to take more than a perfunctory or bureaucratic stance opposing it. But if some students' behavior is merely "negative," "inappropriate," or not up to "expectations," then maybe just the right code of conduct or set of administrative incentives might put everything right.

Increasingly, however, some educational authorities are offering stronger stuff: not just local stand-alone policies but codes or guidelines that reference what appear to be higher and broader authorities. We may feel somewhat encouraged when we see institutional and educational endorsement of documents such as, most notably, the United Nations' Universal Declaration of Human Rights (UDHR). This is neither a trivial nor a regrettable development. The UDHR contains much that any adherent of the Tao would recognize as material fit to be affirmed and taught in our schools. For example, the UDHR's Preamble asserts "recognition of the inherent dignity and of the equal and inalienable rights of all members of the human family [as] the foundation of freedom, justice and peace in the world."[53]

Typically, the teaching materials of a particular school or school system acknowledge the authority of state or provincial codes, also making more extended reference to national codes and in turn to the UDHR. For example, in Canada's most populous province, the Ontario Human Rights Commission offers students and educators a package of materials titled *Teaching Human Rights in Ontario* (2013). This document invokes mainly provincial legislation but also draws attention to the authority (depending on the country) of the Canadian Charter of Rights and Freedoms or of the Constitution of the United States. But beyond these local and national contexts, it also acknowledges the role and status of the UDHR as a foundational document:

> Following World War II, and as a direct result of the human rights atrocities that resulted, the United Nations was formed to protect human rights and stabilize international relations between countries. Its Charter made specific reference to protecting human rights. This was later expanded in the Universal Declaration of Human Rights signed by U.N. member states on December 10, 1948. ... The Declaration is a common standard of conduct for all people and nations. It rises above differing ideologies and philosophies to ensure certain fundamental human rights.

Teaching Human Rights in Ontario traces human rights in the province to the Ontario Human Rights Code. But in addition, the Preamble of this Code "sets the spirit" by situating itself directly in relation to the UDHR, citing the Declaration's claims concerning "the inherent dignity and the equal and inalienable rights of all members of the human family [as foundational for] justice and peace in the world."[54]

We must acknowledge the admirable intentions of Human Rights Codes such as Ontario's and many of the teaching materials that flow from them. Nobody rooted in the Tao could object to the promotion and protection of human rights as such. For these embody, or should embody, or at least reflect, a vision of what it means for human beings to flourish, to fulfill their potential, to cultivate their gifts, to pursue their good purposes, to live lives of meaning and of justice.

Yet such codes are often deficient in a number of ways. A survey of various current human rights codes and guidelines reveals a striking emphasis on a rather narrow set of "thou shalt nots": on the pursuing of complaints about—and the forbidding of—above all, "discrimination and harassment." In much recent usage, this compound phrase almost appears to denote a single thing, or at best to signify a pair of conjoined twins. Again, nobody rooted in the *Tao* will condone harassment in schools or anywhere else. But *discrimination*—a much more complex concept—requires careful discernment. Some readily available human rights documents in places like New Zealand and South Africa are careful to specify "*unfair* discrimination" in their lists of things forbidden. Indeed, we must carefully *discriminate* between forms of fair and unfair discrimination. In school admissions policies, for example, to exclude a student because of his or her race is *unfair* discrimination—and wrong. But to exclude a student because of his or her failure on the entrance examination is arguably a *fair* form of discrimination. Not to make this distinction would be undiscriminating!

However, there is a difficulty still more serious than the wooliness of thought that plagues the language of many human-rights and anti-discrimination documents governing our educational institutions (about which much more could be said). And that is the absence of any true foundation for the ethics upon which these documents *appear* to ground themselves. Our human rights codes may appeal to something such as the UDHR that looks more foundational or universal than something recently passed by the local Provincial Legislature or signed into law in the State House. Yet by itself it is actually not foundational or universal but instead implicitly points to deeper foundations. To say this is not to oppose or trivialize the substance of the UDHR. Far from it. The human rights atrocities of the 1930s and 1940s certainly cried out for some international response, and for a broad, unambiguous commitment to protect human beings from such atrocities. But we need to see that a "universal declaration" is not merely self-referential; it is rooted in the deeper bedrock of the *Tao* (regardless of what we call it), in ultimate sacred postulates which (as indicated in the Appendix, "Illustrations of the *Tao*") have both historical depth and cross-cultural breadth. The UDHR may be silent on the question of its structural and philosophical underpinnings. However, if we read it as an expression of truths real and fundamental, then we needn't dismiss it as a foundation without a foundation.

The problem is not simply that the UDHR is a declaration. As noted in previous chapters, postulates of the *Tao* are just that: postulates, axioms. We misunderstand them if we demand that they have some other kind of underpinning. We have likewise already observed the futility of efforts to ground morality in a supposedly more fundamental substrate, whether that be cast in terms of utilitarianism, or cultural norms, or biology, or evolutionary psychology. In practice, the postulates of the *Tao* do simply need to be declared—but not in a manner that obscures their true universality. One weakness of the UDHR—again, despite its many strengths—is that its authority can appear to derive from the words and decisions of a *political* body. In the language of the Preamble: "The General Assembly proclaims this Universal Declaration of Human Rights as a common standard of achievement for all peoples and all nations."

Even setting aside the hint of circularity in its wording (proclaiming a declaration? declaring a proclamation?), we can see that the document's locus of authority is the UN General Assembly. But of course the Assembly's powers are exercised by its membership, which in turn is a collection of individual representatives appointed by the governments of UN member states. The danger is thus that the General Assembly's *moral* authority may appear to flow from the collective *political* authority of its membership. The GA may thus simply proclaim its Universal Declaration of Human Rights, but in doing so it risks the objection that the document's envisaged *rights* flow from political *might*.

Still more seriously, without a clear and explicit conception of its moral (as distinct from political) foundation or authority, the UDHR was in fact susceptible to attack by those professing moral and cultural relativism, particularly as these professors were represented by the American Anthropological Association (AAA). In late 1947 the Executive Board of the AAA published a "Statement on Human Rights"—a proclamation of its own—which expressed skepticism about the UDHR as it was then taking shape: "How can the proposed Declaration be applicable to all human beings, and not be a statement of rights conceived *only* in terms of the values prevalent in the countries of Western Europe and America?"[55] At one level, of course, this is a fair question. It also illustrates how readily matters of right and wrong can devolve into talk about "values"—which sound as if they might be morally foundational yet emerge on closer inspection as merely local or tribal affairs ("Canadian values," "Texan values," "European values," "liberal values," "conservative values, etc.).[56] But the radically cultural-relativist assumptions of the AAA, if accepted, ensured in principle that, for the UDHR, there *could* be no fair answer.

The AAA "Statement" baldly asserts the "*scientific fact* that no technique of qualitatively evaluating cultures has been discovered." Of course, the response "Then too bad for science!" is not one that the AAA pauses to contemplate. Instead, it declares that in the West what we take to be "eternal verities only *seem* so because we have been taught to regard them as such"; whereas actually, "standards and values are relative to the culture from which they derive so that any attempt to formulate postulates that grow out of the beliefs or moral codes of one culture must to that extent detract from the applicability of any Declaration of Human Rights to mankind as a whole."[57] It's true: every sane person will recognize that cultural bias might influence how we read and apply moral codes. Furthermore, adherence to the *Tao* permits, even invites, a rational discussion about whether a given right specified in the UDHR or any other code is truly universal. But the repeated "only" in the AAA statement, reflecting its creed of cultural and moral relativism, prevents any such discussion from achieving a resolution.

Probably the greatest unconscious irony of the AAA "Statement" is its authors' open abhorrence of the "absolutes in the realm of values and ends" that allegedly underlie Western imperialism and colonialism—the "white man's burden," they are pleased to call these "values"—in combination with their conspicuous confidence in their own ability to know and to judge. It's true that imperialism and colonialism were (and still are) marked by attitudes of moral and cultural superiority. But surely such attitudes are more effectively opposed via a rigorous appeal to the *Tao* than by the smug preaching of the AAA. The anthropologists' professed thoroughgoing relativism is in any case belied by their self-assured statement of faith in what they call "the firm foundation of the present-day scientific knowledge of Man"—by which apparently they mean *their* knowledge!

Little wonder therefore that the AAA "Statement" has functioned since 1947 as something of a Trojan Horse in discussions of universal human rights. Combined with the ambiguity that emerges from the UDHR's rootedness in a political body, doctrinaire cultural relativism offers obvious succor to groups eager to assert *their* political or cultural interpretation of human rights. Most notably, the Cairo Declaration on Human Rights in Islam (1990), signed by (supposed) representatives of 45 states, declares that Sharia Law is the sole source of human rights. Somewhat more equivocally, the Bangkok Declaration (1993) affirms Asian governments' commitment to the UDHR while emphasizing the importance of political and legal non-interference in sovereign states. This Declaration along with other reflections of a so-called "Asian-values" perspective on human rights unmistakably echoes the AAA's nervousness about Western cultural hegemony in standards for human rights. The debates are extensive and ongoing.[58] But what a shame if the purported "firm foundation of ... present-day scientific knowledge" should, as appears, support those who wish to make the UDHR a nose of wax to be twisted according to their own regional, political, ideological, or national agendas.

As already asserted, the aims and substance of the UDHR are deserving of much respect. But unless it is seen as resting on a truly moral rather than ultimately a political foundation, the UDHR remains vulnerable to denials of its claim to universality. Perhaps we needn't go as far as Alasdair MacIntyre's characterization of rights as "moral fictions" among an array of moral fictions that contemporary society trades in. But a similar category suggested by C. S. Lewis might offer a rough fit: that of an "artificial *Tao*," which those whom he calls "the Conditioners" seek to impose for their own purposes.[59]

For again, if the source of a human rights code, whether local or international, is no more than political, then it's not surprising that laws emerging from this "artificial *Tao*" should be driven by the vicissitudes of politics rather than by a deep, genuinely foundational morality. I have emphasized that those grounding themselves in the real *Tao* are or should be open to fresh moral insights. For example, the *Tao* supports, not precludes, historically quite recent realizations concerning the justice of sexual and racial equality. But *Teaching Human Rights in Ontario* is typical in declaring that *its* artificial *Tao*—the Ontario

Human Rights Code—"evolves over time. While the principles of the Preamble remain constant, the way we interpret these principles continues to evolve in step with changes in our society."[60] Adherents of the *Tao* would agree about the need for development and growth in how principles are interpreted, but would deny that such changes should depend on something as fickle and fashion-driven—and as subject to the raw exercise of power—as mere "changes in our society." Sadly, such political and social change can be for better or for worse.

Surely it's reasonable to hope that social change might be driven by interpretation of principles *rather than* that the interpretation of principles should be driven by social change. This critical point cannot be made too strongly. Repeatedly through our discussion we have considered the relationship between might and right. For adherents of the *Tao*—and even for those who *think* they are adherents of the *Tao*—right must always trump might. This is exactly why declarations of human rights are important and necessary: They stand in the face of abuses that arise from an unconstrained exercise of might. It was clear, after the vicious acts perpetrated by totalitarian regimes during the 1930s and 1940s, that something supranational, something "universal" (like the UDHR), was required to protect human beings from such wrongs carried out by those possessing power. Likewise today, it is never enough, when a government or one of its agencies is exposed (for example) to be torturing political prisoners, to say "our national interests require it." For that is ultimately an appeal to a pragmatic and political criterion instead of to one rooted in justice. We are told "We need to do this in order to win" (instead of "in order to practice virtue or actualize the good"). We do not accept this "reason," however. For it is an appeal to might rather than right, and to essentially selfish or local interests rather than to anything universal.

That is precisely why the innocent-sounding claim that interpretation of the principles undergirding human rights codes must evolve in step with societal changes is in fact so pernicious. For such changes are not some neutral or beneficent process that simply unfolds "naturally," with things every day and in every way just getting better and better. As both distant and more recent history attests, not every change in society brings light and enlightenment. Sometimes the changes bring darkness and delusion. Moreover, many such changes are deliberate, chosen, willed. They are not things that merely emerge. They come about because of some party's or some person's open or not-so-open political or educational agenda, one appealed to on the basis of prejudice, or self-interest, or wishful thinking, or desire for group-dominance, or simply false teaching about the nature and purpose of human life.

It is easy to call forth historical examples of such darkness and delusion from Nazi Germany, or the Cultural Revolution in China, or Cambodia under the Khmer Rouge. It is much harder for us to recognize the phenomenon and the tendency when it appears closer to home, in our own countries' present-day politics or schools. But imagine, hypothetically, a human rights code being published in Hitler's Germany or Stalin's Soviet Union with this crucial addendum: "The way we interpret these principles continues to evolve in step with changes in our society." Given the goals and tactics of those controlling the interpretation and enforcing the referred-to social changes, what a vapid and ineffectual code that would be!

Yet what else are many politicians and so-called leaders, including educational thought-leaders, today longing for? Those who hope that the UDHR will regionally be constrained by Sharia Law or by "Asian values" or even by whatever "values" happen to hold sway today in London or Toronto or San Francisco—don't these self-appointed leaders in fact demand *for themselves* the authority, the might, to determine how society changes, and in a way that shields them from any human-rights principles whose interpretation they themselves don't dictate, or does not arise merely in lock-step with social changes they themselves seek to engineer for their own ideological purposes? Such maneuverings to "protect" oneself from the stringent truths of the *Tao* certainly extend deep into the West and aren't characteristic only of regimes in east Asia or in the Muslim world. They are also alive and active in the schools of western Europe, Australia, and North America, of whose ideological trends and self-styled efforts at social change I have barely scratched the surface. Armed with open eyes and a commitment to the *Tao*, however, parents and students can for themselves recognize and penetrate them clearly enough.

For our purposes here, let's simply acknowledge that moralities not based on the *Tao*, not rooted in virtues that transcend politics (including cultural politics), fail to establish the priority of right over might. If in declaring an act or attitude or behavior to be right or wrong I am simply reflecting my emotional state or subjective opinion, then, unless you just happen to share that emotion or subjective opinion, you will not be *morally* persuaded to do the right or to refrain from doing the wrong. Certainly, you might be "persuaded" when you consider the consequences that I threaten to impose, just as the Australian school board mentioned in Chapter 1 might gain compliance to its rules by specifying how it will punish those who smash school furniture. But that is not genuinely moral persuasion. And it's no good appealing to cultural standards according to which one ought not to destroy public property. For cultural "values" are just socially constructed or biologically determined subjectivities raised to a more-than-individual level. To this extent they are still merely contingent on something that is itself not fundamentally moral. They lack an appeal to, or grounding in, what MacIntyre calls "the standards of normative rationality"—and thus they entail an "obliteration of the distinction between manipulative and non-manipulative social relationships."[61] In short, without an appeal to the *Tao*, what pretends to be moral persuasion is really just coercion: might merely *disguised* as right. And so morality is reduced to nothing more than a construct that serves the interests of power.[62]

Another way of saying this is that those denying the Tao or the existence of a truly "normative rationality" render moral standards, precepts, and decisions ultimately *arbitrary*. Usually in common speech, when we call a rule or judgment "arbitrary," we're registering a complaint. We don't like it, because it doesn't seem fair. When we ask "Why should I do what you say?" we're not satisfied with the reply "Because I say so!" We feel coerced, not persuaded. We want to hear a proper reason, not just an appeal to the arbitrary wishes, the *will*, of the person issuing the command or laying down the rule. And of course our term *arbitrary* comes from Latin *arbitrio*, meaning "will." In Chapter 1 we discussed the classical psychology according to which, within a human soul, reason should govern the will and will should in turn guide the passions. But when reason is cut off from the *Tao*, it is rendered ineffectual, removed from true criteria of goodness and justice from which to derive guidance. It is in effect usurped. And will ascends the throne. But this triumph of the will is not something to celebrate. It is a mark not of moral victory but of moral poverty and subjection.[63]

Even when human rights, in their interpretation and application, do *not* fall victim to the exercise of power politics, we should recognize their limitations as a source and support of what Aristotle called *eudaimonia*, "happiness" or human flourishing. This is not to denigrate documents such as the UDHR nor to minimize their importance as protections against abuses of power. Rights codes just by themselves, however, are inadequate as a moral foundation. As stated earlier, such codes may *reflect* a vision of what it means for human beings to pursue good purposes and to live lives of meaning and of justice. To that extent they are harmonious with the *Tao*. But they are no substitute for the cultivation of virtues that arise from the *Tao* and whose exercise positively enacts those purposes and meanings.

To test this claim, let's recall the large issue of *purpose*, or teleology, that is so important in any discussion of moral right and wrong or of human flourishing. Of course, certain kinds of naturalism insist that such questions be taken off the table because they're not "fact-based" or else insufficiently scientific. But by now we've realized we need not let ourselves be coerced into bracketing issues of meaning, purpose, ends. We may boldly demand of any proposal regarding how we should live: What assumptions are you making about the nature and purpose of human beings, about what constitutes the good life? How does your moral framework promote virtues of (for example) beneficence and magnanimity? How does it cultivate human happiness?

This question does not just by itself imply a critique of human rights codes. It's true that the UDHR in particular reminds individuals and governments of the importance of human dignity, security, protection from arbitrary punishment, from enslavement, from suppression of free speech, from interference with parents' "prior right to choose the kind of education that shall be given to their children" (Article 26), and so on. The UDHR thus functions (if adhered to) as a check against wrongs. Yet collectively and individually we need to go beyond protective codes and to cultivate the positively good habits that make for a virtuous citizen or a well-functioning society. Human rights codes identify some behaviors that we must avoid, but merely on their own they impart little *practical wisdom* about the furthering of human happiness, the cultivation of excellent traits of character, the pursuit of worthwhile goals.

Even the wrongs that such codes prohibit are rather limited in scope. Consider the observation of Rosalind Hursthouse and Glen Pettigrove that although our list of generally recognised virtue terms is comparatively short, our list of vice terms is remarkably, and usefully, long ... Much invaluable action guidance comes from avoiding courses of action that would be irresponsible, feckless, lazy, inconsiderate, uncooperative, harsh, intolerant, selfish, mercenary, indiscreet, tactless, arrogant, unsympathetic, cold, incautious, unenterprising, pusillanimous, feeble, presumptuous, rude, hypocritical, self-indulgent, materialistic, grasping, short-sighted, vindictive, calculating, ungrateful, grudging, brutal, profligate, disloyal, and on and on.[64]

Human rights codes may function as a partial brake on a few of these vices, but not many. And turning from vices to their opposite, again we may ask to what extent modern codes foster the venerable classical virtues of prudence (wisdom), temperance (self-control), fortitude (courage), and justice (fairness). Human rights are certainly connected with justice; discrimination and harassment are by their nature not fair. But even adhering scrupulously to the "thou shalt nots" of the codes, a person might still lack wisdom, self-control, courage—and lead a life without a strong sense of meaning and purpose, or even integrity. Then, if we're so bold as to add the theological virtues to our list—faith, hope, love—the scope of human rights appears still more constrained. So once more, the point is not that such codes are useless or contemptible, but only that they do not serve as anything like a sufficient foundation for either private or public morality, or for the kind of human flourishing and sense of purpose that in our hearts most of us long for—and long to see our children cultivate and enjoy.

But without that rootedness in the *Tao*—if the curriculum has nothing more to offer than materials undergirded by political and bureaucratic authorities, or by utilitarianism, or subjectivism, or cultural constructionism, or evolutionary biology—the education of the young lacks an adequate moral foundation.

To begin the mammoth task of reawakening our educational curricula and institutions to the moral challenge we face today, we therefore need to go deeper. So let us rekindle our confidence in the reality of ultimate sacred postulates and unashamedly teach them to ourselves and our children. Not least among the incentives for this process of moral reeducation is the recognition that "virtues benefit their possessor"[65] as well as the wider society in which they are exercised. As citizens, teachers, parents, students—as human with hearts—let us choose moral realism and reject moral nihilism. For moral realism alone empowers us, our children, and our schools to affirm and enrich our common humanity. It alone allows us to ground our lives and our thinking in the *Tao* of right and wrong.

Appendix

Illustrations of the *Tao*

The following pages include virtually all the illustrations of the *Tao* cited by C. S. Lewis in his original appendix to *The Abolition of Man*. However, I have checked all references and quotations, correcting them as required and in numerous cases substituting up-to-date translations.[66] In addition, I have expanded the sample by roughly a third to include sources from other traditions such as Buddhist, Islamic, and Sikh.

As mentioned in Chapter 2, the "axioms" or "ultimate sacred postulates" of the *Tao* appear widely across cultures and across history. The instances cited here—while thus pointing to the reality of the *Tao*, and militating against claims that it is essentially arbitrary or culturally specific—do not themselves *prove* its reality. Yet attestations of its universality are worthy reminders that it *is* real, and so offer at the same time some broad inductive reinforcement against any easy moral skepticism.

Finally, I retain Lewis's categories while emphasizing that their boundaries are not hard and fast; there is much overlap among them. And what follows is of course merely a sample of illustrations, without any pretense of completeness.

The Law of General Beneficence

Negative

"I have not slain men." (Ancient Egyptian. The Confession of the Righteous Soul, "Book of the Dead." *EncycR&E* 5.478)

"You shall not murder." (Ancient Jewish. Exodus 20:13; NIV)

"Abstain from killing living creatures (usually interpreted to mean not killing human beings)." (Buddhist. One of the "Five Precepts"; "pañcaśīla," *PDB* 616.)

"Terrify not men or God will terrify thee." (Ancient Egyptian. Precepts of Ptahhetep. H. R. Hall, *Ancient History of the Near East*, p. 133 n.)

"I saw ... on Nastrond [Corpse-strand, or Hell] ... murderers." (Old Norse. *Völuspá* 38-39)

"I have not brought misery upon my fellows. I have not wrought injuries in the place of right. ... I have not made the beginning of every day laborious in the sight of him

who worked for me. ... I have not impoverished the poor.
I have not done what the gods abominate. ... I have not
caused hunger. I have not caused weeping. I have not
slain. I have not commanded to slay." (Ancient Egyptian.
The Confession of the Righteous Soul, "Book of the Dead."
EncycR&E 5.478)

"Whoso meditates oppression, his dwelling is overturned."
(Babylonian. Hymn to Shamash. *EncycR&E* 5.445)

"If someone, craving his own pleasure, harms harmless
creatures, he will not find happiness anywhere while he is
still alive or after death." (Hindu. *Law Code of Manu* 5.45)

"A man who ... is greedy and deceitful, who deludes the
world, who is given to violence, and who beguiles everybody should be viewed as one who observes the 'cat-vow.'"
(Hindu. *Law Code of Manu* 4.195)

"Greed, like a mad dog, bites anyone and infects all it
touches with a like malady." (Sikh. *Guru Granth Sahib,*
Nat M. 4)

"He, who harbours envy against another, never gathers
Good." (Sikh. *Guru Granth Sahib,* Shloka M. 4)

"Slander not, but speak kindness; speak not evil, but show
good will; whoso slanders and speaks evil—unto him

will [Shamash] requite it by … his head." (Babylonian. *EncycR&E* 5. 446)

"You shall not give false testimony against your neighbor." (Ancient Jewish. Exodus 20:16; NIV)

"Let [one] never use cutting words, show hostility to others in thought or deed, or use aberrant language that would alarm people." (Hindu. *Law Code of Manu* 2.161)

"If one slanders others, he gathers dirt within. If he washes his body from without, the dirt of his mind goes not." (Sikh. *Guru Granth Sahib*, Sri Rag, Var Shloka, M. 3)

"Has he … driven an honest man from his family, broken up a well cemented clan?" (Babylonian. List of sins. *EncycR&E* 5.446)

"Do not impose upon others what you yourself do not desire." (Ancient Chinese. *Analects* 12.2; also 15.24)

"You shall not hate your brother in your heart." (Ancient Jewish. Leviticus 19:17; ESV)

"Do not persist in fighting with thy neighbours." (Ancient Egyptian. *EncycR&E* 5.483)

"Our deeds are the book which the mind writes in the ink (of Desire), and the writing is of two kinds: good and bad." (Sikh. *Guru Granth Sahib,* Maru M. 1)

"Merely set your heart sincerely upon Goodness and you will be free of bad intentions." (Ancient Chinese. *Analects* 4.4)

Positive

"[Nature] prompts men to meet in companies, to form public assemblies and to take part in them themselves; … and to provide a store of things that minister to his comforts and wants—and not for himself alone, but for his wife and children and the others whom he holds dear and for whom he ought to provide." (Roman. Cicero, *De Officiis* 1.4)

"By the fundamental law of nature man [is] to be preserved, as much as possible." (John Locke, *Second Treatise of Civil Government* 2.3.16)

"They love justice and hate violence and robbery." (North American Indigenous. *Jesuit Relations*, 2.73)

"The Master remarked, 'How numerous the people of this state are!' Ran Qiu asked, 'Being already numerous, what can be done to further improve them?' The Master replied,

'Make them wealthy.' 'Once they are wealthy, what else can be done to improve them?' 'Instruct them.'" (Ancient Chinese. *Analects* 13.9)

"People, We created you all from a single man and a single woman, and made you into races and tribes so that you should recognize [or honor] one another." (Islamic. Qur'an, *Al-Hujurat* 49:13)

"See thou of each the light within and ask not his caste." (Sikh. *Guru Granth Sahib,* Asa M.1)

"God commands justice, doing good, and generosity towards relatives and He forbids what is shameful, blameworthy, and oppressive." (Islamic. Qur'an, Al-Nahl 16:90)

"Men ... are born for the sake of men, that they may be able mutually to help one another; in this direction we ought to follow Nature as our guide, to contribute to the general good by an interchange of acts of kindness, by giving and receiving, and thus by our skill, our industry, and our talents to cement human society more closely together." (Roman. Cicero, *De Officiis* 1.7)

"What will explain to you what the steep path is? It is to free a slave, to feed at a time of hunger an orphaned relative or a poor person in distress, and to be one of those who believe and urge one another to steadfastness and compassion." (Islamic. Qur'an, *Al-Balad* 90:12-17)

"I found me another and rich I thought me, / for man is the joy of man." (Old Norse. *Hávamál* 47)

"What good man, what man worthy of the mystic torch … believes that any human woes concern him not?" (Roman. Juvenal, *Satire* 15)

"I am a man: I consider that nothing human is alien to me." (Roman. Terence, *The Self-Tormenter* 1.1)

"You shall love your neighbor as yourself." (Ancient Jewish. Leviticus 19:18; ESV)

"When a stranger sojourns with you in your land, you shall not do him wrong. You shall treat the stranger who sojourns with you as the native among you, and you shall love him as yourself." (Ancient Jewish. Leviticus 19:33-34; ESV)

"Be good to your parents, to relatives, to orphans, to the needy, to neighbours near and far, to travellers in need, and to your slaves. God does not like arrogant, boastful people, who are miserly and order other people to be the same, hiding the bounty God has given them." (Islamic. Qur'an, *Al-Nisa'* 4:37)

"Whatever you wish that others would do to you, do also to them." (Christian. Matthew 7:12; ESV)

"The 'virtuous' and the 'vicious' are not mere words. For, one carries along all that one does." (Sikh. *Guru Granth Sahib,* Jap. 1)

The Law of Special Beneficence

"The gentleman applies himself to the roots. 'Once the roots are firmly established, the Way [*Tao*] will grow.' Might we not say that filial piety and respect for elders constitute the root of Goodness?" (Ancient Chinese. *Analects* 1.2)

"Brothers shall fight and fell each other." (Old Norse. Account of the evil age before the world's end, *Völuspá* 45)

"Has he ... insulted his elder sister?" (Babylonian. List of sins. *EncycR&E* 5.446)

"You will see them take care of their kindred, the children of their friends, widows, orphans, and old men, never reproaching them in the least." (North American Indigenous. Paul Le Jeune, quoted *EncycR&E* 5.439)

"Love thy wife studiously. ... Gladden her heart all thy life long." (Ancient Egyptian. *EncycR&E* 5.481)

"In a man of worth the claims of kinship cannot be denied." (Anglo-Saxon. *Beowulf* [translated by Seamus Heaney], lines 2600-1)

"Be good to your parents and kinsfolk, to orphans and the poor; speak good words to all people." (Islamic. Qur'an, *Al-Baqara* 2:83)

"Did not Socrates love his own children? But in a free spirit, as one who remembers that it was his first duty to be a friend to the gods." (Ancient Greek / Stoic. Epictetus, *Discourses* 3.24)

"Does family affection seem to you to be in accordance with nature and good?—Of course.—What then? Is it possible that, while family affection is in accordance with nature and good, that which is reasonable is not good?— By no means.—That which is reasonable is not, therefore, incompatible with family affection?" (Ancient Greek / Stoic. Epictetus, *Discourses* 1.11)

"I ought not to be unfeeling like a statue, but should maintain my relations, both natural and acquired, as a religious man, as a son, a brother, a father, a citizen." (Ancient Greek / Stoic. Epictetus, *Discourses* 3.2)

"This first I rede thee: be blameless to thy kindred. Take no vengeance even though they do thee wrong." (Old Norse. *Sigrdrifumol* 22)

"[Do] the sons of Atreus alone love their wives? No, every good and sensible man loves and cherishes his wife." (Ancient Greek. Homer, *Iliad* 9.340)

"The interests of society ... and its common bonds will be best conserved, if kindness be shown to each individual in proportion to the closeness of his relationship." (Roman. Cicero, *De Officiis* 1.16)

"We are not born for ourselves alone, but our country claims a share of our being, and our friends a share." (Roman. Cicero, *De Officiis* 1.7)

"Zigong said, 'If there were one able to broadly extend his benevolence to the common people and bring succor to the multitudes ... Could such a person be called Good?' The Master said, 'Why stop at Good? Such a person should surely be called a sage!'" (Ancient Chinese. *Analects* 6.30)

"Do [you] not see that your country is more precious and more to be revered and is holier and in higher esteem among the gods and among men of understanding than your mother and your father and all your ancestors, and that you ought to show to her more reverence and obedience and humility when she is angry than to your father, … and to suffer, if she commands you to suffer, in silence, and if she orders you to be scourged or imprisoned or if she leads you to war to be wounded or slain?" (Ancient Greek. Plato, *Crito* 51a-51b)

"If anyone does not provide for his relatives, and especially for members of his household, he has denied the faith." (Christian. 1 Timothy 5:8; ESV)

"Remind the people to be subject to rulers and authorities, to be obedient, to be ready to do whatever is good." (Christian. Titus 3:1; NIV)

"Repel evil with what is better and your enemy will become as close as an old and valued friend, but only those who are steadfast in patience, only those who are blessed with great righteousness, will attain to such goodness." (Islamic. Qur'an, *Fussilat* 41:34-35)

"I urge … that petitions, prayers, intercession and thanksgiving be made for all people—for kings and all those in authority, that we may live peaceful and quiet lives in all godliness and holiness." (Christian. I Timothy 2:1-2; NIV)

Duties to Parents, Elders, Ancestors

"The father is the embodiment of Prajapati [Protector of Life]; the mother is the embodiment of Earth; ... should someone not attend to [showing them devotion], all his rites bear him no fruit." (Hindu. *Law Code of Manu* 2.226-34)

"Has he despised father and mother?" (Babylonian. List of sins. *EncycR&E* 5.446)

"I was a staff-of-old-age by my Father's side while he was yet upon earth. I went in and out at his command, and transgressed not the utterance of his mouth." (Ancient Egyptian. *EncycR&E* 5.481)

"Honor your father and your mother." (Ancient Jewish. Exodus 20:12; NIV)

"Care of parents." (Ancient Greek / Stoic. List of citizens' duties. Epictetus, *Discourses* 3.7)

"The king should always forgive litigants, children, the aged, and the sick who may insult him." (Hindu. *Law Code of Manu* 8.312)

"Stand up before the gray head and honor the face of an old man." (Ancient Jewish. Leviticus 19:32; ESV)

"I tended the old man, I gave him my staff; I caused aged women to say, 'This is a happy time.'" (Ancient Egyptian. *EncycR&E* 5.481)

"You will see them take care ... of old men." (North American Indigenous. Le Jeune, quoted *EncycR&E* 5.439)

"I have not taken away the oblations of the blessed dead." (Ancient Egyptian. The Confession of the Righteous Soul, "Book of the Dead," *EncycR&E* 5.478)

"Take great care in seeing off the deceased and sedulously maintain the sacrifices to your distant ancestors, and the common people will sincerely return to Virtue." (Ancient Chinese. *Analects* 1.9)

Duties to Children and Posterity

"Marriage, begetting children." (Ancient Greek / Stoic. List of citizens' duties. Epictetus, *Discourses* 3.7)

"Can you imagine an Epicurean State? One man says, "I do not marry." "Neither do I," says another, "for people ought not to marry." No, nor have children; no, nor perform the duties of a citizen. ... Where are the citizens to come from? Who will educate them? Who will be superintendent of the [young army recruits], or gymnasium director? Yes, and what will either of these teach them?" (Ancient Greek / Stoic. Epictetus, *Discourses* 3.7)

"Nature ... implants in [man] above all ... a strangely tender love for his offspring." (Roman. Cicero, *De Officiis* 1.4)

"Do not kill your children for fear of poverty—We shall provide for them and for you—killing them is a great sin." (Islamic. Qur'an, *Al-Isra'* 17:31)

"If we will face the facts, we shall find that there have been many instances of achievement in peace more important and no less renowned than war." (Roman. Cicero. *De Officiis* 1.22)

"You owe the greatest reverence to the young." (Roman. Juvenal, *Satire* 14)

"The Master said, 'We should look upon the younger generation with awe.'" (Ancient Chinese. *Analects* 9.22)

"The killing of the women, and more especially the killing of the young boys and girls who are to go to make up the future strength of the ... people, is the saddest part ... and we feel it very sorely." (North American Indigenous. Account of the 1890 Wounded Knee Massacre. Quoted in *EncycR&E* 5.432)

The Law of Justice

Sexual justice

"Has he intruded upon his neighbour's house, approached his neighbour's wife?" (Babylonian. List of sins. *EncycR&E* 5.446)

"I have not lain with a married woman. I have not committed impurity." (Ancient Egyptian. The Confession of the Righteous Soul, "Book of the Dead." *EncycR&E* 5.478)

"You shall not commit adultery." (Ancient Jewish. Exodus 20:14; NIV)

"Do not go anywhere near adultery; it is an outrage, and an evil path." (Islamic. Qur'an, *Al-Isra'* 17:32)

"Evil the eyes that feed on the beauty of another's woman." (Sikh. *Guru Granth Sahib,* Asa M. 1, Var Shloka M.1)

"Abstain from engaging in sexual misconduct." (Buddhist. One of the "Five Precepts"; "pañcaśila," *PDB* 616.)

"I saw … on Nastrond [Corpse-strand, or Hell] … workers of ill with the wives of men." (Old Norse. *Völuspá* 38-39)

"Where women are revered, there the gods rejoice." (Hindu. *Law Code of Manu* 3.56)

Honesty

"Has he used an unjust balance, taken base money? ... drawn false boundaries?" (Babylonian. List of sins. *EncycR&E* 5.446)

"I have not stolen. ... I have not done crookedness." (Ancient Egyptian. The Confession of the Righteous Soul, "Book of the Dead." *EncycR&E* 5.478)

"The king should exert the utmost effort in suppressing thieves." (Hindu. *Law Code of Manu* 8.302)

"You shall not steal." (Ancient Jewish. Exodus 20:15; NIV)

"Evil the hands that grab what is another's." (Sikh. *Guru Granth Sahib,* Asa M. 1, Var Shloka M.1)

"Prefer a loss to a dishonest gain." (Ancient Greek. Chilon, Fragment 10, cited in Diogenes Laertius, *Lives* 1.3)

"Abstain from taking what is not given." (Buddhist. One of the "Five Precepts"; "pañcaśīla," *PDB* 616.)

"Justice is the constant and perpetual desire to give to each one that to which he is entitled." (Roman. Justinian, *Institutes* 1.1)

"[We] made a list of all persons we had harmed, and became willing to make amends to them all; [and] made direct amends to such people wherever possible, except when to do so would injure them or others." Alcoholics Anonymous, steps 8 and 9.

"If the native made a 'find' of any kind, such as a honey tree, and marked it, it was thereafter safe for him, as far as his own tribesmen were concerned, no matter how long he left it." (Indigenous Australian. *EncycR&E* 5.441)

"The first office of justice is to keep one man from doing harm to another, unless provoked by wrong; and the next is to lead men to use common possessions for the common interests, private property for their own. There is, however, no such thing as private ownership established by nature, but property becomes private either through long occupancy (as in the case of those who long ago settled in unoccupied territory) or through conquest ... or by due process of law, bargain, or purchase, or by allotment." (Roman. Cicero, *De Officiis* 1.7)

Justice in court, etc.

"Whoso takes no bribe, but makes intercession for the weak, well pleasing is this to [Shamash]." (Babylonian. Hymn to Shamash. *EncycR&E* 5.445)

"I have not traduced the slave to him who is set over him."
(Ancient Egyptian. The Confession of the Righteous Soul,
"Book of the Dead." *EncycR&E* 5.478)

"You shall not give false testimony against your neighbor."
(Ancient Jewish. Exodus 20:16; NIV)

"A man must either not enter the court or speak candidly;
by refusing to speak or by speaking deceitfully, he com-
mits a sin." (Hindu, *Law Code of Manu* 8.13)

"Regard him whom thou knowest like him whom thou
knowest not." (Ancient Egyptian. *EncycR&E* 5.483)

"You shall do no injustice in court. You shall not be partial to the poor or defer to the great, but in righteousness
shall you judge your neighbor." (Ancient Jewish. Leviticus
19:15; ESV)

The Law of Good Faith and Veracity

"A sacrifice is lost by telling a lie about it." (Hindu. *Law
Code of Manu* 4.237)

"Those who work evil, their seed has not continuance;
whose mouth, full of lying, avails not before thee. Thou
burnest their utterance, rendest it asunder." (Babylonian.
Hymn to Shamash. *EncycR&E* 5.445)

"With his mouth was he full of Yea, in his heart full of Nay? Is it because of the injustice that he meditated in order to disperse the righteous, to destroy [them], to wrong, to rob, to cause to be robbed, to have dealings with evil?" (Babylonian. List of sins. *EncycR&E* 5.446)

"I have not spoken falsehood." (Ancient Egyptian. The Confession of the Righteous Soul, "Book of the Dead." *EncycR&E* 5.478)

"Abstain from lying." (Buddhist. One of the "Five Precepts"; "pañcaśīla," *PDB* 616.)

"[I] never fomented quarrels, never swore to a lie." (Anglo-Saxon. *Beowulf* [translated by Heaney], lines 2738-39)

"The Master said, 'Be sincerely trustworthy and love learning, and hold fast to the good Way [*Tao*] until death.'" (Ancient Chinese. *Analects* 8.13)

"We know the Truth when the heart is True, … We know the Truth when we love the Truth. … We know the Truth, when our Soul knows the Way." (Sikh. *Guru Granth Sahib,* Vadhans M. 3)

"I saw … on Nastrond [Corpse-strand, or Hell] treacherous men." (Old Norse. *Völuspá* 38-39)

"I hate that man like the gates of Hades' house who conceals one thing in his heart, but says another." (Ancient Greek. Homer. *Iliad* 9.305)

"The foundation of justice ... is good faith—that is, truth and fidelity to promises and agreements." (Roman. Cicero, *De Officiis* 1.7)

"Truth is the highest of all Virtues; but higher still is the living of Truth." (Sikh. *Guru Granth Sahib,* Sri Rag M. 1)

"Let your actions be governed by dutifulness and trustworthiness." (Ancient Chinese. *Analects* 1.8)

"Everything is better than being with the deceitful." (Old Norse. *Hávamál* 126)

The Law of Mercy

"The children, the aged, the feeble, and the sick are to be regarded as the rulers of space." (Hindu. *Law Code of Manu* 1.184)

"Has he failed to set a prisoner free, or not loosed one who was bound?" (Babylonian. List of sins. *EncycR&E* 5.446)

"I have given bread to the hungry, water to the thirsty, clothes to the naked, a ferry boat to the boatless." (Ancient

Egyptian. The Confession of the Righteous Soul, "Book of the Dead." *EncycR&E* 5.478)

"One should never strike a woman, not even with a flower." (Hindu. Paul Janet, *Histoire de la Science Politique* 1.8)

"There, Thor, you got disgrace, when you beat women." (Old Norse. *Harbarthsljoth* 38)

"In the Dalebura tribe, a woman, a cripple from birth, was carried about by the tribes-people in turn until her death at the age of sixty-six. ... They never desert the sick." (Indigenous Australian. *EncycR&E* 5.443)

"You will see them take care of ... widows, orphans, and old men, never reproaching them in the least." (North American Indigenous. *EncycR&E* 5.439)

"When Nature gave tears to man, she proclaimed that he was tender-hearted; and tenderness is the best quality in man." (Roman. Juvenal, *Satire* 15)

"They said that of all the kings upon the earth he was the man most gracious and fair-minded." (Anglo-Saxon. Praise of the hero in *Beowulf* [translated by Heaney], lines 3180-81)

"When you reap your harvest in your field and forget a sheaf in the field, you shall not go back to get it. It shall be for the sojourner, the fatherless, and the widow." (Ancient Jewish. Deuteronomy 24:19; ESV)

The Law of Magnanimity

"There are ... two kinds of injustice—the one, on the part of those who inflict wrong, the other on the part of those who, when they can, do not shield from wrong those upon whom it is being inflicted." (Roman. Cicero, *De Officiis* 1.7)

"Men always knew that when force and injury was offered they might be defenders of themselves; they knew that howsoever men may seek their own commodity, yet if this were done with injury unto others, it was not to be suffered, but by all men and by all good means to be withstood." (English. Richard Hooker, *Laws of Ecclesiastical Polity*, 1.10)

"To take no notice of a violent attack is to strengthen the heart of the enemy. Vigour is valiant, but cowardice is vile." (Ancient Egyptian. The Pharaoh Senusert III, cited in H. R. Hall, *Ancient History of the Near East*, p. 161)

"They came to a land of joy, the pleasant lawns and happy seats of the Blissful Groves. ... Here is the band of those who suffered wounds, fighting for their country." (Roman. Virgil, *Aeneid* 6.638-39, 660)

"Spirits must be the harder, hearts the keener, courage the greater, as our strength grows less. Here lies our lord all hacked to pieces, a good man in the dust. He will mourn evermore who thinks to turn back from this war-play now." (Anglo-Saxon. *The Battle of Maldon* 312-16)

"Praise and imitate the one who, though he loves life, is not grieved to die." (Roman / Stoic. Seneca, *Letters* 54)

"The Master said, 'Be sincerely trustworthy and love learning, and hold fast to the good Way [*Tao*] until death." (Ancient Chinese. *Analects* 8.13)

"When the stress of circumstances demands it, we must gird on the sword and prefer death to slavery and disgrace." (Roman. Cicero, *De Officiis* 1.23)

"A warrior will sooner die than live a life of shame." (Anglo-Saxon. *Beowulf* [translated by Heaney], lines 2890-91)

"We must not follow those who advise us, being men, to think on human things, and, being mortal, of mortal things, but must, so far as we can, make ourselves immortal, and strain every nerve to live in accordance with the best thing in us; for even if it be small in bulk, much more does it in power and worth surpass everything." (Ancient Greek. Aristotle, *Nicomachean Ethics* 1177B)

"The soul then ought to conduct the body, and the spirit of our minds the soul. This is therefore the first law, whereby the highest power of the mind requireth general obedience at the hands of all the rest concurring with it unto action." (Richard Hooker, *Laws of Ecclesiastical Polity* 1.8)

"[He] who is unmoved, who has restrained his senses ... is said to be devoted. ... As a light standing in a windless (place) flickers not, [so is the devoted]." (Ancient Indian. *Bhagavad Gita. EncycR&E* 2.90)

"This means nothing else than that [the soul] pursued philosophy rightly and really practised being in a state of death: or is not this the practice of death?" (Ancient Greek. Plato, *Phaedo* 81a)

"I trow I hung on that windy Tree / nine whole days and nights, /stabbed with a spear, offered to Odin, / myself to mine own self given." (Old Norse. *Hávamál* 137)

"Very truly I tell you, unless a kernel of wheat falls to the ground and dies, it remains only a single seed. But if it dies, it produces many seeds. Anyone who loves their life will lose it." (Christian. John 12:24-25; NIV)

Sources
The Bible:

NIV: Scripture quotations marked (NIV) are taken from the Holy Bible, New International Version®, NIV®. Copyright © 1973, 1978, 1984, 2011 by Biblica, Inc.™ Used by permission of Zondervan. All rights reserved worldwide. www.zondervan.com. The "NIV" and "New International Version" are trademarks registered in the United States Patent and Trademark Office by Biblica, Inc.™

ESV: English Standard Version® (ESV®) Copyright © 2001 by Crossway, a publishing ministry of Good News Publishers. All rights reserved. ESV® Text Edition: 2016.

Confucius, *Analects*, translated by Edward Slingerland. Indianapolis: Hackett Publishing, 2003.

Encyclopedia of Religion and Ethics, edited by James Hastings et al. 12 vols. Edinburgh: T. & T. Clark, 1908-1921. [Abbreviated *EncycR&E.*]

The Law Code of Manu, translated by Patrick Olivelle. Oxford: Oxford University Press, 2004.

The Princeton Dictionary of Buddhism, edited by Robert E. Buswell Jr. and Donald S. Lopez Jr. Princeton: Princeton University Press, 2013. [Abbreviated *PDB*]

The Qur'an, translated by M. A. S. Abdel Haleem. Oxford: Oxford University Press, 2004.

Sri Guru Granth Sahib: An Anthology, translated by Gopal Singh. Calcutta: Birla Foundation, 1989.

Notes

In the following notes, authors and/or works appearing in **bold face** also appear in the Further Reading section, where their full publication details may be found.

1. See, for example, Paul Bloom's fascinating study of moral judgments made by babies before the age of language acquisition: *Just Babies: The Origins of Good and Evil* (New York: Broadway Books, 2013). Such babies, Bloom shows, exhibit strong disapproval of unkind, bad-guy puppets and approval of kind, nice-guy puppets. However, because these preferences can't be explained in terms of language or culture, Bloom concludes that the babies' moral "capacities for judgment and feeling" are "natural"—that is, "a legacy of our evolutionary history" (p. 99). Bloom does not ponder the role of anything that might go even deeper than, or beyond, nature or nurture.

2. www.ereadingworksheets.com/reading-worksheets/fact-and-opinion.htm.

3. See Dennis Danielson and Christopher M. Graney, "The Case Against Copernicus," *Scientific American* 310.1 (January 2014): 72-77.

4. David Wootton, *The Invention of Science: A New History of the Scientific Revolution* (New York: Harper Collins, 2016), p. 254. Wootton's entire 59-page chapter titled "Facts" (pp. 251-309) richly illustrates how complex and relatively recent is the history of this familiar concept.

5. For a further critique of the fact/opinion distinction, see Justin McBrayer's video presentation, "Why The Fact Opinion Dichotomy is Harmful," www.youtube.com/watch?v=jQnY-iGTHi_0, along with his *New York Times* editorial (see Further Reading).

6. **Lewis, *Abolition***, pp. 16-17.

7. **MacIntyre 1981**, pp. 13-14, 25.

8. www.edu.gov.on.ca/extra/eng/ppm/128.pdf.

9. www.education.vic.gov.au/school/teachers/studentman-agement/Pages/studentbehaviour.aspx.

10. www.apelslice.com/books/9780618843175NIMAS/HTMLOUT/HTML/c_id4632222.html.

11. One of the most famous debates focusing on "interested," power-based "constructions" of morality took place in 1971 between American linguist Noam Chomsky and French deconstructionist Michel Foucault, who coined the phrase "regimes of truth" to suggest that power underlies not only right and wrong but also truth itself. Among innumerable sites, see for example www.critical-theory.com/noam-chomsky-argues-foucaults-ghost/. And for a video in which Chomsky declares that "there are no moral relativists," see www.youtube.com/watch?time_continue=124&v=i63_kAw3WmE.

12. www.jewishencyclopedia.com/articles/7436-heart.

13. See *An Encyclopedia of Philosophy*, ed. G. H. R. Parkinson (London: Routledge, 1988), 464; also plato.stanford.edu/entries/ancient-soul/#3.2.

14. **Milbank and Pabst**, pp. 7, 4.

15. **Lewis, *Abolition***, p. 24.

16. Alan Bloom, *The Closing of the American Mind* (Simon & Schuster, 1987), 133.

17. **Milbank and Pabst**, p. 5.

18. plato.stanford.edu/entries/emotions-17th18th/LD8Hume.html#ReaOugOnlSlaPas; plato.stanford.edu/entries/hume-moral/.

19. **Lewis, *Abolition***, p. 25.

20. Grant, in **Cayley**, p. 82.

21. Augustine, *City of God*, XV.22; www.ccel.org/ccel/schaff/npnf102.pdf.

22. *Centuries of Meditations* 1.12; www.ccel.org/t/traherne/centuries/cache/centuries.pdf.

23. Aristotle, *Nicomachean Ethics* 1104B and 1095B: www.perseus.tufts.edu/hopper/text?doc=Perseus%3Atext%3A1999.01.0054%3Abekker%20page%3D1104b; and www.perseus.tufts.edu/hopper/text?doc=Perseus%3Atext%3A1999.01.0054%3Abekker%20page%3D1095b.

24. Roy A. Rappaport, *Ritual and Religion in the Making of Humanity* (Cambridge: Cambridge University Press, 1999), 359. See also A. Berriedale Keith, "Righteousness (Hindu)," *Encyclopedia of Religion and Ethics*, vol. 10.

25. From "Striving for Unity: A Conversation with Roy Rappaport"; quod.lib.umich.edu/cgi/t/text/text-idx?cc=mdia;c=mdia;c=mdiaarchive;idno=0522508.0016.104;rgn=main;view=text;xc=1;g=mdiag.

26. Bhavna Malik, "Educational Philosophy of the Gurus – The making of Mankind," sikhinstitute.org/july_2013/2-bhavna.html.

27. "Taoism or Daoism" and "Tao," *The Concise Oxford Dictionary of World Religions*.

28. Alain de Lille, *Complaint of Nature*, Prose 3; legacy.fordham.edu/halsall/basis/alain-deplanctu.asp.

29. Grant, in **Cayley**, p. 154.

30. This cynical position dates from ancient times. In Plato's *Republic*, the character Thrasymachus declares justice to be merely the advantage of the stronger members of society, those who make the rules and enforce them to their own advantage (*Republic* 344c).

31. I borrow the phrase from Richard Winter, "Post-Modern Sociology as a Democratic Educational Practice? Some Suggestions," *British Journal of Sociology of Education* 12.4 (1991): 467-481: "'Modernism', as a category, is a vacuous self-congratulation, implying that historical periods (e.g. 'Medieval', 'Renaissance', 'Classical',) have led up to this, here, now: *we* (at last) have explanations which we know to be eternal so we need envisage no further periodization—to be 'modern' is to be 'up-to-date', sufficient" (p. 471).

32. **Lewis, *Abolition*,** p. 42.

33. **Lewis, *Abolition*,** p. 44; italics added.

34. T. H. Huxley, "Evolution and Ethics" (The Romanes Lecture), available at archive.org/details/evolutionandethi-00huxluoft. All quotations of Huxley are from this site.

35. Eila K. Roberts et al., "A Bruce Effect in Wild Geladas," *Science* 335 (9 March 2012): 1222-1225.

36. See Rosalind Hursthouse's stimulating discussion of reason as it concerns differences between humans and other animals: "In virtue of our rationality—our free will if you like—we are different. ... There is no knowing what we *can* do from what we *do* do, because we can assess what we do do and at least try to change it"; **Hursthouse**, p. 221. We don't assume that Geladas can rationally assess their behaviors and align them with standards of ethics. But as Hursthouse affirms, "we are different." And as the poet John Milton wrote concerning humankind, "Reason also is choice"; *Paradise Lost* 3.108.

37. For further discussion, see my article "The Logic of Pope's Optimism," *Christianity and Literature* 34.3 (1985): 23–36.

38. **Lewis, *Abolition*,** pp. 45-46.

39. *Analects,* translated by Edward Slingerland (Indianapolis: Hackett Publishing, 2003), *12.5.*

40. Terence, *The Self-Tormentor*, 1.1.

41. *Second Treatise of Civil Government*, chap. 3. For other examples, see Appendix.

42. Of course the conventions of mathematical notation and the like are socially constructed, but not the truths these are used to express.

43. *Analects*, 15.40.

44. www.publicbooks.org//nonfiction/where-do-morals-come-from.

45. "Cultural Relativism and Universal Human Rights," *AnthroNotes* (Smithsonian Institution), 20.2 (Winter 1998); anthropology.si.edu/outreach/anthnote/Winter98/anthnote.html.

46. One of the liveliest recent presentations of consequentialism is *The Moral Landscape*, by Sam Harris. Pulizer-Prize-winning novelist and public intellectual Marilynne Robinson negatively reviewed Harris's book in the *Wall Street Journal* www.wsj.com/articles/SB1000142405274870388240457552006 2380030080 and from the self-anointed champion of reason and science evoked the thin-skinned accusation that her review was "paranoid, anti-science gabbling." See www.samharris.org/blog/item/response-to-critics-of-the-moral-landscape.

47. Only if science is an all-or-nothing enterprise claiming for itself a universal jurisdiction can the position I am sketching here be slandered as "anti-science." No true assertor or

defender of the *Tao* will despise enlightenment offered by the contributions of psychology, sociology, evolutionary biology, empirical brain science, and so on. What such a one will refuse is the claim that these fields are just by themselves sufficient to define, ground, and illuminate matters of right and wrong.

48. *De Officiis* 1.7.

49. Because of the current dominance of this second sense of "nature," I avoid linking the *Tao* (as it is sometimes linked) with the tradition or philosophy of "Natural Law."

50. *The First Three Minutes: A Modern View of the Origin of the Universe* (New York: Basic Books, 1977), p. 154.

51. The overly simplifying or "reductionist" tendencies of physics are sometimes parodied in various apocryphal stories about physicists who promise to predict the winner of any given horse race—but with the proviso that the race must involve perfectly elastic spherical horses moving through a vacuum.

52. A notable and well written defense of hard naturalism's capacity to satisfy the human desire to access sources of meaning and morality is offered by Sean Carroll, who tries to brighten up naturalism with adjectives such as "poetic," "dramatic," "dynamic," even "cheerful." But beginning from strictly naturalistic premises, Carroll concludes (of course) that the source of "oughts" and values "isn't the outside world; it's inside us." And so "The world, and what happens in the world, matters. Why? Because it matters to me. And to you." Moreover, "our ethical systems are things that are constructed by us human beings." **Carrol, *The Big Picture*,** pp. 389, 393, 405.

53. The full document may be accessed at www.un.org/en/universal-declaration-human-rights.

54. www.ohrc.on.ca/sites/default/files/Teaching%20 Human%20Rights%20in%20Ontario_2013.pdf, pp. 2, 41, 65, 66, 80.

55. The Executive Board, American Anthropological Association (AAA), "Statement on Human Rights," *American Anthropologist*, New Series 49.4, Part 1 (Oct.-Dec. 1947): 539-543 (p. 539, italics added).

56. George Grant offers a devastating critique of "values talk," which often sounds as if it connects with deeper sources of morality but in practice relativizes right and wrong by divorcing "values" from deep considerations of purpose and treating them as mere creations of individual or community choice, of raw arbitrary will. And thus, "the language of value is above all the language of Nietzsche. ...Once you have gotten rid of the universe of meaning, then everything becomes our making, our willing, our choosing" (Grant, in **Cayley**, pp. 121-122). For a more recent intriguing discussion of liberal and conservative "values," see Jonathan Haidt, *The Righteous Mind: Why Good People Are Divided by Politics and Religion* (New York: Vintage, 2013).

57. AAA, "Statement on Human Rights," p. 542 (italics added).

58. There is a huge literature on human rights. Its history, arguments, and complexities far exceed the purposes and limitations of this short book.

59. **MacIntyre 1981**, pp. 91-92; **Lewis, Abolition,** p. 74.

60. *Teaching Human Rights in Ontario*, p. 6.

61. **MacIntyre 1981**, pp. 28-29.

62. This stark view is openly that of an entire influential school of moral philosophy from Friedrich Nietzsche in the nineteenth century (*Beyond Good and Evil, The Genealogy of Morals, The Will to Power,* and elsewhere) to Michel Foucault

and his postmodernist followers in the 1980s and beyond. See (among many others) the discussion offered by **Charles Taylor**, pp. 586-600.

63. *Triumph of the Will*, not incidentally, is the apt title of Leni Riefenstahl's famous 1935 propaganda film about the Nazi party congress in Nuremberg, celebrating Hitler's consolidation of power in Germany.

64. **Hursthouse and Pettigrove**, p. 20.

65. See the chapter titled "The Virtues Benefit their Possessor," in **Hursthouse**, pp. 163-191.

66. Of course it is worth keeping in mind that any translation runs the risk of "cultural appropriation." Yet what would the state of our knowledge be without translation?

Further Reading

The following short but heterogeneous list of works suggests places to begin a further study of moral philosophy. (Some of them have bibliographies of their own which might facilitate still further study.) Not all the approaches represented in the books or articles cited here harmonize fully, or even approximately, with that of *The Tao of Right and Wrong*. But for convenience I have starred five works of (broadly) moral realism that I recommend with particular enthusiasm.

Anscombe, G. E. M. 1958. "Modern Moral Philosophy." *Philosophy* 33:124.

Bloom, Alan. 1987. *The Closing of the American Mind: How Higher Education Has Failed Democracy and Impoverished the Souls of Today's Students.* New York: Simon & Schuster.

Brooks, David. 2015. *The Road to Character.* New York: Random House.

Carroll, Sean. 2016. *The Big Picture: On the Origins of Life, Meaning and the Universe Itself.* London: Oneworld. Especially chapters 44-50.

*Cayley, David. 1995. *George Grant in Conversation.* Toronto: House of Anansi Press.

Foot, Philippa. 2002. *Virtues and Vices: And Other Essays in Moral Philosophy.* New York: Oxford University Press.

Harris, Sam. 2011. *The Moral Landscape: How Science Can Determine Human Values.* New York: Free Press.

*Hursthouse, Rosalind. *On Virtue Ethics.* 1999. Oxford: Oxford University Press.

*Hursthouse, Rosalind and Glen Pettigrove. "Virtue Ethics." *The Stanford Encyclopedia of Philosophy* (Winter 2016 Edition). Edward N. Zalta (ed.). plato.stanford.edu/archives/win2016/entries/ethics-virtue/.

*Lewis, C. S. 1943. *The Abolition of Man.* Rpt. New York: Macmillan, 1965.

———. 1967. "The Poison of Subjectivism." In *Christian Reflections.* London: Bles.

MacIntyre, Alasdair. 1967. *A Short History of Ethics.* Rpt. London and New York: Routledge, 1998.

*———. 1981. *After Virtue: A Study of Moral Theory.* Rpt. London: Bloomsbury, 2016.

McBrayer, Justin P. "Why Our Children Don't Think There Are Moral Facts." *New York Times*, 2 March 2015. opinionator.blogs.nytimes.com/2015/03/02/why-our-children-dont-think-there-are-moral-facts/?_r=0.

Meilaender, Gilbert. 2010. "On Moral Knowledge." In *The Cambridge Companion to C. S. Lewis*, pp. 119-131. Cambridge: Cambridge University Press.

Milbank, John, and Adrian Pabst. 2016. *The Politics of Virtue: Post-Liberalism and the Human Future*. London: Rowman & Littlefield.

Parfit, Derek. 2011. *On What Matters*. 2 vols. Oxford: Oxford University Press.

Rappaport, Roy A. 1999. *Ritual and Religion in the Making of Humanity*. Cambridge: Cambridge University Press.

Sasse, Ben. 2017. *The Vanishing American Adult: Our Coming-of-Age Crisis—and How to Rebuild a Culture of Self-Reliance*. New York: St. Martin's Press.

Scruton, Roger. 2017. *On Human Nature*. Princeton: Princeton University Press.

Sinnott-Armstrong, Walter. "Moral Skepticism." *The Stanford Encyclopedia of Philosophy* (Fall 2015 Edition). Edward N. Zalta (ed.). plato.stanford.edu/archives/fall2015/entries/skepticism-moral/.

Smith, James K. A. 2014. *How (Not) to Be Secular: Reading Charles Taylor*. Grand Rapids: Eerdmans.

———. 2016. *You Are What You Love: The Spiritual Power of Habit*. Grand Rapids: Brazos Press.

Taliaferro, Charles. 2010. "On Naturalism." In *The Cambridge Companion to C. S. Lewis*, pp. 105-118. Cambridge: Cambridge University Press.

Taylor, Charles. 2007. *A Secular Age*. Cambridge, MA: Harvard University Press.

Wojtyła, Karol Józef (Pope John Paul II). 1993. *The Splendour of the Truth* (*Veritatis Splendor*). www.catholic-pages.com/documents/veritatis_splendor.pdf.

Author's Note and Acknowledgments

I originally conceived of this book as a twenty-first-century tribute to C. S. Lewis's *The Abolition of Man*—a kind of "remake" of Lewis's pithy challenge to educators issued seventy-five years ago, in 1943. For readers who know *The Abolition*, the family resemblance of this book will still be obvious enough. However, I hope they will also have sensed how my own book has grown in the writing to engage numerous issues and strains of thought quite different from those Lewis was tackling in his own time and context.

I don't recall when I first read *The Abolition of Man*, but I remember the first time I taught it: four decades ago, when, as a PhD student in English at Stanford, I was given a class of twenty undergraduates in what was then called Freshman English. One standard early exercise in that course was a précis of an assigned expository text; after that, we'd move on to more interesting forms of writing. But I wanted my students to start with something intellectually meaty, so I asked them to read *The Abolition*, which after all was a deep but accessible set of three moral essays written by an English professor. Students were instructed to produce a three-hundred-word summary of the first chapter—not an exciting or creative assignment, but one I felt would get them writing and thinking. I was surprised, however, at my students' keen interest in what Lewis actually had to say. It seemed to touch a nerve and feed a hunger. In those days before the Web or Amazon. com, one eager young man named Casey even asked me where he could buy an extra copy as a Christmas present for his mother.

Now, decades later, I'm less certain that *The Abolition* is as accessible to students and teachers as it once was. Yet I'm still convinced that those involved in the education of young people, including young people themselves, need to hear the message of moral realism. My aim in *The Tao of Right and Wrong,* therefore, has been not only to refashion and reframe Lewis's argument but also to update his examples in an idiom more familiar to today's readers than something originally written in 1943—though not to "dumb down" his argument, nor to offer a mere paraphrase, and certainly not to produce a scholarly discussion *about* it. No short book should try to "cover the waterfront." Lewis's didn't, and neither does this one. I've accordingly avoided the standard academic practice of engaging in "discussion about discussions" (valuable as that can be) and in heavy footnoting and referencing of the works of others. All this parsimony was intended to keep *The Tao of Right and Wrong* approximately as compact as Lewis's book was, with only three chapters and an appendix.

I offer my deepest appreciation to those who have read all or parts of earlier drafts of this book. It (and I) have benefited immensely from both their kindness and their critique. Thank you to Dan Balow, John Danielson, Nora Danielson Lanier, Will Danielson Lanier, Carolyn Lanier, Mark Lanier, Carey Newman, Bill Reimer, Margaret Somerville, and above all my beloved life partner, Janet Henshaw Danielson. Faults aplenty may remain in spite of others' generous help, and for these I alone am responsible.

CPSIA information can be obtained
at www.ICGtesting.com
Printed in the USA
LVHW04*2133150618
580393LV00001BA/1/P